"In *The Strengths-Based Workbook for Stress Relief*, Niemiec shows how your strengths can be a resource both for joy and resilience. This workbook will help readers craft a more meaningful and rewarding life, whether they are seeking to amplify what's good in their lives or find a way through difficult times."

—**Kelly McGonigal, PhD**, author of *The Upside of Stress* and *The Willpower Instinct*

"I've worked for decades at the intersection of mind-body health, healing, and stress management. Ryan Niemiec's book championing the use of character strengths to manage stress is a milestone in mind-body wellness, the first of its kind. It offers a template for shifting how you think about and handle your daily stress. This book is a well-being booster, a resilience enhancer, and a stress manager all in one! At the least, you'll be freshly empowered to handle your future stressors; and at best, you'll transform your life while uplifting those around you."

—**Joan Borysenko, PhD**, *New York Times* bestselling author of *Minding the Body, Mending the Mind*

"In this groundbreaking workbook, Ryan Niemiec takes the reader on a journey of discovery, providing help in identifying their stress and character strengths. This process is linked to a range of excellent tools to tackle stress. At the end of each chapter the Learn, Practice, SHARE section assists in embedding what has been learned. This easy-to-read, positive psychology–informed book takes a self-coaching approach and promotes personal growth and development. This book could possibly change your life."

—**Stephen Palmer PhD**, professor of practice at the Wales Institute for Work-Based Learning at the University of Wales Trinity Saint David, founder and director of the Centre for Stress Management, and coauthor of *How to Deal with Stress*

"This book is a breakthrough addition to the field of health and wellness. Taking the newest insights from psychology, Niemiec shows how to turn stress from our enemy into our friend. This book is a game changer."

—**Sean Slovenski**, president of Health and Wellness, Walmart

T0301144

"*The Strengths-Based Workbook for Stress Relief* provides practical, research-based strategies we can all use to manage the stresses of daily life by using our particular character strengths to cope most effectively, no matter the situation. Readers will not only come away with a solid understand of the science underlying these strategies, but also have the opportunity to directly practice implementing these techniques in their own lives through a series of easy-to-follow guided exercises throughout the book. This engaging workbook is therefore a must-read for anyone who feels overwhelmed by the chaos of daily life and struggles to find happiness."

> —**Catherine A. Sanderson, PhD**, Manwell family professor of life sciences in the
> department of psychology at Amherst College, and author of *The Positive Shift*

"As a coach working with clients who face a daily struggle with anxiety and stress, I cannot think of a better way to empower them to find their own path to better mental health than to offer them *The Strengths-Based Workbook for Stress Relief.* We all face stress and struggles. When stressed, it is hard to imagine that we already have what we need to make things better. Often, we look outside for the source of our stress and for the cure. And yet research shows that we all have innate capacities that help us navigate life's ups and downs and to handle pressure. *The Strengths-Based Workbook for Stress Relief* is your guide to discovering and reinforcing those capacities to create a life in which you manage your stress instead of your stress managing you!"

> —**Ruth Pearce, ACC, JD, PMP**, coach, project motivator, and author of
> *Be a Project Motivator*

The

STRENGTHS-BASED
WORKBOOK
for
STRESS RELIEF

A Character Strengths Approach *to* Finding Calm *in the* Chaos *of* Daily Life

RYAN M. NIEMIEC, PsyD

New Harbinger Publications, Inc.

Publisher's Note

Distributed in Canada by Raincoast Books

Copyright © 2019 by VIA Institute on Character
New Harbinger Publications, Inc.
5674 Shattuck Avenue
Oakland, CA 94609
www.newharbinger.com

Cover design by Sara Christian

Acquired by Wendy Millstine

Edited by Cindy B. Nixon

Library of Congress Cataloging-in-Publication Data on file

Printed in the United States of America

21   20   19

10   9   8   7   6   5   4   3   2   1   First Printing

for

my Maya

my daughter,

illusion – dreams – love – generous – princess – great – water – God's creative power

each of these meanings is in your universal name, originating across the world's cultures,

you are, at once, all of these

and you transcend them all

Contents

Foreword

Stress is a fact of life for us all. It can be a killer, causing physical, psychological, and spiritual damage. And it can be a catalyst to personal growth and hardiness. A key question in our personal and collective quests for happiness and fulfillment is how to turn stress into our ally instead of our enemy. This book breaks new ground in helping us do this better.

Ryan Niemiec, PsyD, reframes the way we look at stress. Instead of viewing it primarily as something we need to avoid and eliminate, he uses the newest insights into human psychology to help us grow from our stress. If that's not enough, this book also helps us become mindful about *creating* the kinds of challenges that help us become strong, resilient, and fulfilled. In so doing, the author describes what can be termed "constructive stress"—a new and promising approach to health and well-being.

This book presents new scientific insights into positive personality elements, called "character strengths," that reside in all of us. There are 24 of them. Their presence transcends all of our differences—whether those be in culture, gender, race, ethnicity, or religion. These strengths are configured uniquely within each of us, resulting in the singular character profiles that are so important to personal identity. We all share common facial elements, like eyes, ears, mouths, noses, and eyebrows, and yet these elements configure differently on everyone, giving us each a distinct physical appearance. Such are the character strengths, revealing our unique character profiles.

Recent science has begun to uncover just how broadly these strengths apply to our well-being, to achievement of our goals, and to elevating the common good. By directing our attention from what's wrong to what's strong, we discover overlooked potential in ourselves and others, and we escape the downward spiral of feeling hopeless and helpless in the face of life's challenges. Instead, we discover the opportunity that lies within both our smallest and our greatest challenges.

With heightened awareness of these powers within, we can become more effective at deploying them to *cope* with stressful circumstances. Many great examples of this are provided throughout this book. Awareness of our own strengths and the character strengths of others can also help us *avoid* many stressors by helping us make better life choices, whether those choices have to do with the work we choose to do, the relationships we choose to be in, or how we find meaning and fulfillment. Building a flourishing life on the foundation blocks of our character strengths helps us become hardier and more resilient when we encounter the very toughest challenges of life.

This book represents a breakthrough addition to the field of stress by providing a science-based lens through which we can view stress as opportunity. It helps us become "psychological martial artists" by neutralizing a strong negative force coming at us and turning it into a more positive purpose. In a world in which so many of us feel overwhelmed and somewhat lost, and in which there are so many forces causing stress and advising us in so many directions, we now have a clear and practical workbook that simplifies things and empowers us to become our best selves and to help others do the same. With this, Dr. Niemiec has handed the world a compass to navigate to our highest and best potential—to find calm in the storms of life. Use this book. Wear it out. And share it with those you care about most.

—Neal H. Mayerson, PhD
Chair, VIA Institute on Character

Your Strengths Can Reduce Stress

What's the first thing that comes to mind when you think of "stress"? For me, my mind turns to feeling overwhelmed at work. I'm a hard worker, I don't mind putting in the extra hours. I think about work during time off. I say yes to many (perhaps too many) proposals and interesting projects, regardless of how full my plate already is. This is a recipe for stress.

I feel the stress in my body like a weight pressing against me from behind. And a sense of anguish arises when I have thoughts like, *How am I going to get all of this done? Why do I keep taking on so much?* I sometimes feel helpless (*I can't do all of this!*) or frustrated (*Dammit, why am I doing this to myself?*) or agitated when someone comes to me with a new request.

If I'm not careful, this work stress bleeds into my relationship with my wife, making me on edge in my communication with her, which in turn leads her to be more sensitive around me. Then, of course, our children feel the impact as well—either sensing the tension or noticing my absence when I'm working.

Pervasiveness of Stress and Strength

Stress comes in big forms, such as divorce, job loss, injury, illness, or death of a loved one, that can take a gigantic toll on our physical and mental well-being. Stress also comes in small forms, such as traffic on the way to work, a lingering cough, a crying child, a messy room that has to be cleaned up. The potential for experiencing stress lies in every situation of our day.

We're also subject to the unplanned pileup of stressful events or experiences. For example, I might be feeling busy and confident at work, but then I take on a couple new projects that have to be juggled with driving my kids to several activities throughout the week. On top of that, my wife gets sick, my sister needs some extra support due to a breakup, and the friend from whom I typically get my own support has to cancel our plans at the last minute. Before I know it, I find myself in a heap of stress. And as stressors build and build, coping resources dwindle.

As you think about your own stress, do you notice the pileup effect of stressful events? Do you see the large and small dosages of stress in your life? It can be interesting to notice that anything in your life can be a potential stressor—good things can stress us out, and even boredom or being lost in routine can be a hidden stressor.

It's also interesting to note that what's particularly stressful for one person (like house-cleaning) can be uplifting for another. Driving in traffic can fill one person with rage and can ruin the rest of their day while another can use the situation as an opportunity to listen to an audiobook, call a friend, or relax to music—they're actually grateful that they've been slowed down so they can appreciate these other activities. With big stressors such as divorce, there are seemingly countless complex tensions and an array of struggles that arise; although these struggles are challenging, some people are able to see them as opportunities for new growth and learning while others seem to crumble and deteriorate at each new stressor that comes around the corner.

How do you respond to stress?

Thankfully, there are new resources that can empower us to manage stress and approach it in a different way. As you will discover in this book, just as stress can be all-encompassing, emerging in small and large doses, and can have an overwhelming effect on us, we can say the same about our strengths. There is a hidden power that lies within you that emerges as your strengths of character. Strengths come in small and large forms and can have a transformative effect on you. They can also have small effects, whereby the benefits subtly build each day. In other words, your strengths, like your stressors, can pile up too! The reality is that within any situation—the positive, the negative, the mundane—there are strengths to be discovered and used.

We're Stressed by What's Wrong

As human beings, we are wired to emphasize "what's wrong." We are quick to be hard on ourselves when we make mistakes, to negatively size someone up because of their political or religious views, to see weaknesses in others, and to notice something inconsistent in our environment that might signal danger. This is sometimes referred to as having a "negativity mind-set." Although there are protective elements in these examples, this can contribute substantially to our stress levels.

In short, focusing on what is wrong more than on what is strong stresses us out. For example, in the early 2000s, a research team led by scientist Roy Baumeister (2001) set out to look for instances in which "good" was stronger than "bad." They asked:

- Are positive emotions like love and gratitude stronger than upsetting emotions like anger and sadness?

- Do positive relationships have a bigger impact on us than bad relationships?

- Are areas such as good parenting and good health more impactful than bad parenting and bad health?

Unfortunately, no. For every situation the researchers examined, they came to the same conclusion: "bad is stronger than good." Anger and sadness will likely stick with you and impact your behavior more than joy and love because positive emotions bounce off you like a trampoline and negative emotions stick with you like glue.

It can be unsettling to acknowledge this. I know the feeling firsthand. One of the scenarios the researchers looked into was good versus bad feedback. I, like so many others, can give a presentation to fifty people and receive forty-nine glowing reviews and only one negative comment—but which do you think I focus on? Per the research finding, bad feedback has a stronger pull on us, and so I'll give little attention to the positive remarks of forty-nine different people to instead concentrate on the one critic.

This research highlights an important point: we need to create more balance between the positive and the negative. To do this, the challenge in many cases is to accentuate the positive, see the good in the person you are with, build upon your own strengths, express appreciation, and learn from the positives of your past. Your strengths can help you counterbalance your negativity bias. Whereas attending to the negative is important for growth and is an important theme of this book, you need to not forget about what is going right with you.

Returning to the example of my presentation feedback, when I look at the situation objectively, I can see that my behavior, while common for public speakers, is absurd. I have forty-nine opportunities to build upon the positive, understand my strengths from a wide range of perspectives, and capitalize on more of the good that people witnessed, but instead, I single out that one outlier. This creates more stress for myself, as if to say, "If I can learn from what that one person sees wrong, maybe I can get 100 percent of the audience to like my presentation next time." The moral of the story is that we should attend to both sides of the equation, making adjustments accordingly *and* giving priority to where the positive energy is.

Going with the positive, however, is easier said than done. There are a number of stress factors that pull against this. Here are some sobering research statistics:

- More than 75 percent of people in the United States are not flourishing (Keyes 2002). A large portion are languishing, which is a form of stress that means going through the motions in life without high psychological or social well-being.

- Seventy percent of American workers are not engaged with their work (Gallup 2013). This means that the majority of workers are not reaching their full potential. People are disengaged for a number of reasons, and many are actively disengaged, which means they are doing things that negatively impact their work (skipping meetings, being dishonest with their boss).

- Sixty-seven percent of people do not have a meaningful awareness of their strengths (Linley 2008). If a person is unaware of who they are, how can they be expected to build good relationships, be successful at work, and do well in life? I refer to strength unawareness as "strengths blindness" and argue that 100 percent of people have blind spots about their strengths (Niemiec 2014). No person is fully aware of their strengths or has full self-knowledge.

- In one study of thousands of workers, those who reported they used their strengths a lot were eighteen times more likely to be flourishing than those who reported using their strengths very little (Hone et al. 2015). But the majority of people in this study were not flourishing.

These issues of flourishing, languishing, strengths blindness, and strengths engagement will be explored in this book. From chapter to chapter, it will become clear to you that your strengths are pathways to what is most important in your life. It's as if you have an internal "lever" that you can pull to create a healthy balance between attending to what's wrong and appreciating what's strong—a lever that allows you to see the good within a fog of stress, a lever that propels you to greater well-being.

Common Humanity of Strengths

In the late 1990s, psychologists were realizing that, over the previous century, there had been far more research and attention on problems, disorders, and negative psychology than on the positive aspects of life, such as strengths psychology, virtues, and well-being. One researcher at the time, David Myers (2000), calculated the gap between studies published on positive emotional experiences (such as happiness) and studies published on negative emotional experiences (sadness, anxiety). He discovered that for every one study on positive experiences, there were twenty-one studies on the opposite. Wow, what an imbalance in the field!

Something needed to change—not to replace the negative, but to bring the positive on an equal footing in terms of the science. The leader of this wave of thinking was Martin Seligman. As president of the prestigious American Psychological Association, he wanted to bring about a shift in the field and thus called for a "positive psychology" (1999). He challenged researchers and mental health professionals to examine the plus side of life and to not only understand how to bring a client who is suffering back up to a level of nonsuffering, but to investigate how we might bring a person from normal functioning to flourishing. In other words, on a scale from 1 to 10, rather than moving someone from −7 to 0, how do we move a person from a 2 or 3 to a 9 or 10?

Seligman offered a framework for the field of positive psychology as the study of positive emotions, positive traits, and positive institutions. Meanwhile, Neal Mayerson, a practicing psychologist and philanthropist at the time, was intrigued by the area of positive traits. He picked up the phone and called Seligman (whom he'd never met), and the two of them hit it off. They decided they could work together to advance the study of positive traits. They initiated a process in which Seligman would recruit top scientists in the field and Mayerson would offer thought leadership and funding support through the Mayerson Foundation, a family philanthropy based in Cincinnati.

Throughout the first year of their collaboration, they met with top scientists and leaders on the themes of virtue, character, and strengths to hear about the latest thinking and program developments. At one meeting, a realization reverberated among the members: we can't really talk about this work because we don't have a common language to communicate with one another about positive qualities. So Chris Peterson, a distinguished professor at the University of Michigan, was chosen to lead a team of fifty-five scientists to investigate a handful of questions. What is best about human beings? What are the most important traits, or qualities, that are in us? What characteristics are found in every person, across the globe?

It was the year 2000, and the researchers went to work. They wanted to learn about any philosopher, theologian, or organization that had written about virtues, ethics, strengths, or positive qualities. They reviewed the writings of ancient Greek philosophers (such as Aristotle and Plato), closely surveyed all of the world's main religions (the big five being Christianity, Buddhism, Islam, Judaism, and Hinduism), and examined the works of virtue writers over the centuries, such as King Charlemagne, Saint Thomas Aquinas, and Benjamin Franklin. Early positive thinkers such as Marie Jahoda and Abraham Maslow were reviewed. Organizations that have ways of framing virtues, such as the Boy Scouts and Girls Scouts, were examined. Not wanting to leave any stone unturned, they also looked at the strengths and virtues found in eulogies, on tombstones, in greeting cards, and even in popular culture, such as in the fictional Klingon language in *Star Trek*.

What the researchers discovered was that there were six common themes that ran across the major philosophies and religions:

- Wisdom

- Courage

- Humanity

- Justice

- Temperance

- Transcendence

These became the virtues of what was named the "VIA Classification" (of what is now known as the VIA Institute on Character), with *via* meaning "the way" or "the path" in Latin. The team then applied a variety of scientific criteria to determine the character strengths that would nest under these virtues, such criteria as: Is the strength measurable? Is it valued or morally valued? Are there institutions that build it up? Is it found across cultures? It is fulfilling in and of itself?

Part of this process involved testing the strengths across countries and continents (Park, Peterson, and Seligman 2006). In addition, the researchers traveled to remote areas of the world to interview people who had not interacted much with modern civilization, like the Maasai of Kenya and the Inuit of Greenland (Biswas-Diener 2006). These populations were asked about the strengths and whether they were valued in their culture, had institutions to build them, and so forth. Remarkably, these character strengths did exist across cultures, countries, and belief systems. It appeared that what was emerging was a universal set of positive characteristics in human beings.

This three-year research process resulted in the VIA Classification of Character Strengths and Virtues from the VIA Institute (see http://www.viacharacter.org/www/Character-Strengths; Peterson and Seligman 2004), shown in the table below, which classifies 24 human strengths grouped under the six overarching virtues and provides definitions for each.

The VIA Classification of Character Strengths and Virtues

Virtues	Definitions	Character Strengths	Definitions
Wisdom	Thinking-oriented strengths that help you build knowledge	Creativity	You are viewed as a creative person. You see, do, and/or create things that are of use. You think of unique ways to solve problems and be productive.
Wisdom		Curiosity	You are an explorer. You seek novelty. You are interested in new activities, ideas, and people. You are open to new experiences.
Wisdom		Judgment/ Critical Thinking	You are analytical. You examine things from all sides. You do not jump to conclusions, but instead attempt to weigh all the evidence when making decisions.
Wisdom		Love of Learning	You often find ways to deepen your knowledge and experiences. You regularly look for new opportunities to learn. You are passionate about building knowledge.
Wisdom		Perspective	You take the "big picture" view of things. Others turn to you for wise advice. You help others make sense of the world. You learn from your mistakes.
Courage	Emotional or gut-oriented strengths that help you dig deep with an issue and face adversity	Bravery	You face your fears and overcome challenges and adversity. You stand up for what is right. You do not shrink in the face of pain or inner tension or turmoil.

Virtues	Definitions	Character Strengths	Definitions
Courage		Perseverance	You keep going and going when you have a goal in mind. You attempt to overcome all obstacles. You finish what you start.
Courage		Honesty	You are a person of high integrity and authenticity. You tell the truth, even when it hurts. You present yourself to others in a sincere way. You take responsibility for your actions.
Courage		Zest	You are enthusiastic toward life. You are highly energetic and activated. You use your energy to the fullest degree.
Humanity	Strengths that help you connect with others, and tend and befriend people	Love	You are warm and genuine to others. You not only share but are open to receiving love from others. You value growing close and intimate with others.
Humanity		Kindness	You do good things for people. You help and care for others. You are generous and giving; you are compassionate.
Humanity		Social Intelligence	You pay close attention to social nuances and the emotions of others. You have good insight into what makes people "tick." You seem to know what to say and do in any social situation.
Justice	Strengths that help you build and connect with the larger community	Teamwork	You are a collaborative and participative member groups and teams. You are loyal to your group; you feel a strong sense of duty to your group. You always do your share.

Virtues	Definitions	Character Strengths	Definitions
Justice		Fairness	You believe strongly in an equal and just opportunity for all. You don't let personal feelings bias your decisions about others. You treat people the way you want to be treated.
Justice		Leadership	You positively influence those you lead. You prefer to lead than to follow. You are very good at organizing and taking charge for the collective benefit of the group.
Temperance	Strengths that help you manage your vices and prevent excess	Forgiveness	You readily let go of hurt after you are wronged. You give people a second chance. You are not vengeful or resentful. You accept people's shortcomings.
Temperance		Humility	You let your accomplishments speak for themselves. You see your own goodness but prefer to focus the attention on others. You do not see yourself as more special than others. You admit your imperfections.
Temperance		Prudence	You are wisely cautious. You are planful and conscientious. You are careful to not take undue risks or do things you might later regret.
Temperance		Self-Regulation	You are a very disciplined person. You manage your vices and bad habits; you stay calm and cool under pressure. You manage your impulses and emotions.

Virtues	Definitions	Character Strengths	Definitions
Transcendence	Strengths that help you connect outside yourself and make sense of the larger universe	**Appreciation of Beauty & Excellence**	You notice the beauty and excellence around you. You are often awestruck by beauty, greatness, and the moral goodness you witness. You are often filled with wonder.
Transcendence		Gratitude	You regularly experience and express thankfulness. You don't take the good things that happen in your life for granted. You tend to feel blessed in many circumstances.
Transcendence		Hope	You are optimistic, expecting the best to happen. You believe in and work toward a positive future. You can think of many pathways to reach your goals.
Transcendence		Humor	You are playful. You love to make people smile and laugh. Your sense of humor helps you connect closely with others. You brighten gloomy situations with fun and jokes.
Transcendence		Spirituality	Your life is infused with a sense of meaning and purpose. You feel a connection with something larger than yourself. Your faith informs who you are and your place in the universe. You maintain a regular spiritual and/or religious practice.

What's particularly exciting about this classification is that it marks the first time in history that there is a "common language" for talking about strengths of character—a substantive common language for understanding, exploring, researching, and using qualities that are positive and essential in human beings.

Stress Can Unleash Character Strengths

Let's look more closely at the term "character strengths." Character strengths are positive parts of your personality that define who you are and help you reach positive outcomes. They make up what is best in you—when you are at your best, your character strengths are right there helping you along the way. When you are suffering—overcome by stress, facing difficult emotions, or lost in an argument with a loved one—your character strengths can be unleashed. Consider these three examples:

- Jacob was stressed about a new procedure his sales team had taken on. Each team member was instructed by the manager to sell as many products as possible, and the results would be posted at the end of each day for all to see. Jacob's teammates were particularly competitive with one another, each person jockeying and manipulating to try to be the top seller. He found that as the competition increased, some team members became more hostile. Others were distant and avoidant. This led to increased tension in the workplace. Some days, Jacob dreaded going to work. *Not one more day,* he thought. The stress got so high that he considered looking for a new job. Before taking that step, though, he decided to use his top strength, curiosity, at work. For Jacob, this meant asking questions and showing a genuine interest in his teammates. He was careful to not ask questions that might lead the team to think he was fishing for an advantage, so he asked about their life in general, their weekend plans, their hobbies and interests. This approach catalyzed a friendlier, more open environment. The team began to spend more time together, including work breaks and lunches. The edginess of the stress smoothed out. Although competition still reigned, it became a topic of humor and fun, rather than a cutthroat win-or-lose approach.

- When Micah was a child, she wanted to rescue every feral and wounded animal she came across. She knew all the contact information for the animal shelters and veterinarians in her area and made use of each one. Sometimes she went out of her way to help wild animals that appeared injured, such as fallen birds or small animals caught in a piece of human garbage. Micah would become upset when she was unable to help an animal. This strong nurturing instinct inspired her to become an ER nurse. It sustained her in the demands of the job and the daily situations of discomfort she faced. Micah explained that her strength of kindness has been the driving force in her life, propelling her to thoroughly enjoy her life and always look to how she might be able to help those who are suffering.

- Chris and Erin have a strong marriage. Their best times in the past fifteen years had always come when they were together—traveling, having dinner with friends, going to theme parks, and cuddling up with a movie. When they had conflicts, they seemed to quickly turn to peacefulness, talking it through, compromising, and complimenting each other. As they considered which strengths contributed to their happy marriage, they both agreed, without hesitation, that for Chris, it was his self-regulation; he was adept at managing any impulse to say something hurtful during arguments, and he was committed to disciplined, harmonious, and thoughtful conversations amid tension. For Erin, it was her forgiveness. She was a natural at being able to let go of Chris's personal quirks and bad habits. She took this approach to their tense conversations as well, in which she would listen carefully, share her perspective, and then let it all go.

In each example, it is clear that character strengths are central to the person's identity—they make each person stronger and more competent when faced with challenges and tensions. And the strengths lead to some kind of benefit—for the person's achievement or for the relationship or the work environment. These examples show that our character strengths are an important ingredient in bringing benefit to others and to improving ourselves.

Research in the years since the VIA Classification emerged has been very positive, amounting to well over five hundred scientific studies published on the classification (see https://www.viacharacter.org/www/Research/Research-Findings) and the VIA Survey, which is a tool that measures the strengths in individuals and which is discussed further in chapter 2 (see the "Understanding Your Strengths Profile" section). The application of character strengths has also taken off as these strengths are being used in such various settings as organizations, universities, schools, clinics, hospitals, and even correctional facilities.

Research studies show that character strengths can lead to the following outcomes:

- Greater levels of flourishing

- More resilience

- Less distress

- Improved coping with stress

- More positive emotions

- Higher engagement with activities

- Increased life meaning

- Higher work productivity, job satisfaction, and work engagement

- Stronger and more intimate relationships

This book will help you discover how your character strengths can serve as pathways to these areas to help enhance your well-being and manage your stress. As you soon will discover, your strengths are there, waiting to be used.

My Journey with Strengths

My formal journey with these character strengths started when the classification came out in the mid-2000s. At the time, I was a clinical psychologist helping hundreds of people a year who were struggling with a wide range of stressors, including feelings of overwhelm as a parent, relationship stress, struggles in managing a new medical diagnosis, spiritual stress (a lack of life meaning and purpose), and depression- and anxiety-related stress. I helped each person zero in on what was wrong and how they might improve their life. I focused quite a bit on their suffering—how the stress came about, why it continued, and how to manage it better. I attempted to bring in character strengths, but at the time there was minimal guidance on how to do so. Then, in 2004, when the VIA Classification was published, opportunity knocked. Now there existed a "common language" to discuss strengths, to frame conversations, and to offer a different slant on interventions. My clients began to use the language and soon realized they had far more resources within them than they previously knew.

Suddenly, my clients and I were on the exact same page. When I asked them how they'd used their strengths with a stressor in the last week, they had an answer! They knew where I was coming from. They could say they'd used curiosity to look at the problem in a fresh way or perseverance to overcome obstacles in the way of reaching a goal. And since this system was based in science, it no longer felt "forced" or uncomfortable for me to suggest a gratitude or curiosity exercise. These strengths simply became part of our conversation, as well as part of homework activities to practice between meetings. But there was more than that. These character strengths became part of their personal growth and inner transformation.

I didn't stop there. I couldn't! I felt pulled toward this compelling work that seemed to offer something particularly unique to the world—cutting deep to who we are as human beings. It was something I wanted to be part of. Therefore, in 2009, I was privileged to be appointed the education director of the nonprofit VIA Institute on Character, which initiated this work and has continued to not only steward but also advance the science and practice of character strengths each day. In this role, I began to spend the majority of my time steeped in the science and practice. To this day, I research, practice, teach, personally apply, write, and discuss these character strengths with people around the world. It's my full-time job!

Along the way, as I write books, scientific articles, and blogs, and give keynote addresses and workshops, stress has been at my side, sometimes lifting me up, sometimes trying to drag me down. Character strengths, however, reveal the positive side of stress—they remind us that we are stronger than we realize and that we have substantial capacity to be resilient and to flourish. I have taken that message to heart.

How to Use This Workbook

This workbook is specifically designed to help you identify your stress and your strengths and to offer you new, guiding tools for approaching your stress and using your strengths. I recommend working through the book in sequence, as each chapter builds on the last one and flows into the next. As you proceed, you may find the following elements supportive.

Journaling

I like to refer to a quote often attributed to Aristotle: "You are what you repeatedly do." To paraphrase, the action (or inaction) you put forth in life is you. That's your identity. We can make that strong and positive. An important part of this is creating good habits. Journaling is one way to take this action.

As such, space is allotted throughout this book to reflect on and explore various activities. Additionally, you might find it useful to keep a separate "Strengths and Stress" journal in the form of a pocket notebook, a smartphone app, or a computer file in which you can delve further into the concepts, research, and exercises. This will help you maintain good habits.

Self-Insight

Research has shown that whereas reflecting on and evaluating your thoughts, feelings, and behaviors is important for stress resilience, self-insight is even more beneficial for handling stress (Cowden and Meyer-Weitz 2016; Grant, Frankline, and Langford 2002). Self-insight refers to being aware of your thoughts, feelings, and behaviors, and understanding why you feel and behave in certain ways. This book emphasizes both—awareness and insight—particularly with the aim of more easily moving you in the direction of positive change once you have catalyzed new insights.

Your Strengths Practice

Engaging in strengths practices is an essential way to become more aware of and competent with your character strengths. Each chapter will offer you a number of activities to try. The practices in these sections are meant to be completed in the moment *and* practiced regularly in your daily life. Keep practicing the ones you enjoy. Make them part of your daily routine. For your convenience and repeated use, a selection of these activities can be found online at http://www.newharbinger.com/42808.

Meditations

Chapter 8 provides descriptions and links to special audio meditations you can access. These are strengths-based meditations designed to enhance your understanding of the ideas and activities in this book. They offer you tools you can practice with and use each day.

Learn. Practice. SHARE.

At the end of each chapter, you'll find a section titled "Learn. Practice. SHARE." This idea builds off a model of learning shown to be most effective in shifting our behavior or mind-set (McGonigal 2015). It involves following a process of building and taking in new knowledge and ideas (learn); experimenting, exploring, reflecting, and taking action with the knowledge and ideas (practice); and then passing along your learning or coexploring this work with others (share).

Throughout each chapter, you'll be delving into plenty of learn and practice activities; therefore, these concluding sections are meant to remind you to share your experience with others, face-to-face or by social media, phone, or any method of connecting with others. For example, you might engage in one of the activities with someone, have a discussion about a certain topic, share news about your findings, or help them practice some of the material on strengths and stress.

Grateful Ending, Hopeful Beginning

I will conclude this introduction and encourage you forward with two of my own top strengths. First, I am grateful to be in a position to offer you these insights and experiences. It is a true honor. I have experienced plenty of stress in my life, and I have received tremendous benefit from using the tools of positive psychology—namely, character strengths—to address this stress. Second, I am hopeful for you as you begin this journey. I'm confident this work with strengths will deepen your relationship with others and your personal insights. It will help you achieve more, reach your goals, and find more confidence and meaning in your life. May you find wide application and benefit from this work.

Let's continue our journey.

CHAPTER 1

Your Current Stress and Well-Being Levels

When Mike was diagnosed with lung cancer, he was stunned. How could this be? He was only forty-five years old and he had been a nonsmoker his whole life. *Cancer...me...really?* he thought. He was married with two young children he wanted to see grow up and find success and meaning in the world. He was working for a major company and was rising up the corporate ladder, making it to midlevel management the previous month with a substantive raise. And suddenly, out of nowhere, his doctor gave him this news that left him speechless and worried. His life had seemed to finally be coming together in a good way—like all the puzzle pieces that had once been scattered were now fitting neatly into place—and now everything was scrambled again. Needless to say, his stress was high. Mike's diagnosis, coupled with the increasing demands of his new job and the continual needs of his kids, brought him to a breaking point.

As Mike talked more with his medical team, he learned that he was lucky to be in the early stages of the disease and that his five-year survival rate was approximately 50 percent. Still, part of him felt as if he could see the finish line of his life. He consulted other professionals and began to do research, mostly on the Internet. He was surprised to hear a couple stress experts say that stress is an opportunity and something that can be viewed in a positive way. *No way,* Mike thought. *That's both insensitive and insulting for them to say that! Clearly, they've never had real stress. If they did, they wouldn't say that.*

It turns out, those experts were right. We'll return to Mike later in this chapter.

What Are Your Stress Levels?

Before we dig into the nature of stress and ways to approach it, let's pause for a moment to review your life areas and experiences and explore your current stress levels in different situations.

Using the form below, write down ten to fifteen situations—big and small—in which you feel stress. Consider all the domains of your life, such as work, school, family, relationships, health, parenting, leisure, community, and spirituality. Be sure to write about *specific* situations; for example, not just *My job,* but *Giving a presentation at the weekly team meeting* or *Interacting with Jody on the big marketing project.* In the area of relationships, you might write, *Calling my dad because he is sick and agitated* or *Getting in the door after work and managing my kids' snacks, homework, and transition from school.*

After each specific example, write down the intensity level of the stress you typically experience in that situation on a scale from 1 to 10, where 1 and 2 indicate a very mild, low-intensity level of stress and 9 and 10 reflect a very strong, high-intensity level of stress. Although there are three columns for these ratings, fill out only the first one for now. You'll be invited to return to the other columns later in this workbook.

Specific Situation	Start (rating 1–10)	Mid (rating 1–10)	End (rating 1–10)
When I share a comment at the monthly community meeting in my neighborhood	7		
When I log on to social media and don't see many "likes" or comments on my pictures and posts	3		

This is not meant to be a formal assessment; rather, it's a way for you to take stock of your current stressors and stress levels. Now that you have identified your stressors and how much they affect you, let's try an experiment.

Your Stress Mind-Set

Consider two points of view, or mind-sets: "Stress is harmful" and "Stress is helpful." Here are some statements associated with each mind-set:

1. Stress is harmful:

    *   Stress blocks my learning, growth, and productivity.

    *   Stress worsens my health and zest level.

    *   Stress should be avoided because its effects are negative.

2. Stress is helpful:

    *   Stress enhances my learning, growth, and productivity.

    *   Stress improves my health and zest level.

    *   Stress should be used because its effects are positive.

Write down which of the two statements you agree with more strongly. Is it "Stress is harmful" or "Stress is helpful"?

_____

Consider the reason(s) you chose that statement. Jot down the first things that come to your mind:

_____

_____

If you're like most people, you think stress is harmful. Stress is generally thought of as bad—something negative that hurts us. In part, this is because stress has gotten a bad rap over the years. And some of that is for good reason. There's no doubt that stress can hurt us, negatively impacting us on all levels—physical, mental, emotional, social, and spiritual. Too much stress, called *distress* or *chronic stress,* can bring on certain diseases and disorders, make existing pain and chronic illnesses worse, and lead to such problems as anxiety, depression, isolation, and burnout.

Chronic stress and poor coping are connected not only with bad health, but also with worsening relationships, decreased concentration, and a host of other negative effects. You might notice that you speak of stress from a perspective of being upset, such as, "I'm so stressed and exhausted today from all this extra work my boss gave me" or "I just can't handle my kids anymore—they're climbing up the walls, and I'm so stressed!" Many of us picture stress as a big black blob that takes over us and crushes our body and mind. When you're upset, you can feel it in your body's physiology through such means as an increased heart rate, a headache, shallow breathing, tightened muscles, light-headedness, or nausea. It's uncomfortable to feel stress.

Research studies show that stress is most likely to be harmful if, because of stress, you feel inadequate, you feel out of control or a sense of meaninglessness, or you isolate from others (McGonigal 2015). I have reframed these three categories as the "three H's" of stress risk: helplessness, hopelessness, and hiding. Given all this, how can stress possibly be good for us?

Stress researchers like Alia Crum and Kelly McGonigal at Stanford University have been examining stress and the mind-sets associated with it for years. They offer statements and beliefs about stress to their research subjects, similar to those you just read. Then they test their subjects on several measures, such as how well the individuals manage their stress, how high their well-being levels are, physiological indicators like levels of stress hormones in their body, and various measures of life functioning.

What they consistently find is that people who believe that stress is helpful are more satisfied in life, less depressed, more productive and happy at work, and have greater confidence that they can cope with life challenges. They find more meaning in the struggles of life (McGonigal 2015).

You might be skeptical about this. Have the people who find stress helpful simply experienced less stress in their lives, as Mike suggested at the start of this chapter? Researchers have examined that possibility as well and have found that people with both mind-sets experience suffering and stress equally. In other words, stress is a ubiquitous part of life that cannot be omitted for anyone. *We all have stress, but we don't all have the same mind-set about it.*

Can Stress Really Be Something Positive?

Stress is a fundamental requirement for growth. Mike came to this realization a few months after sitting in the hospital exam room receiving his initial diagnosis. But it did not come easy. Shortly after leaving the hospital, Mike felt his world was crashing down on him and he became depressed. He tried to spend constant time with his wife and kids, as if to cling to every moment he had left with them, although his focus wasn't there. His body was there, but his mind wasn't paying much attention. The other areas of his life weakened. He took a medical leave from his job, so a primary source of personal meaning and accomplishment vanished. He disconnected from his friends and disengaged from his hobbies and sport activities. His sadness level was at an all-time high, he spent far too much time in bed, and he felt unfocused. He was riddled with worry about his family's future and his impending doom. Yet even though he stopped participating in so many activities and therefore had more time, it didn't change his stress level. In fact, he felt worse. Mike was caught in the *narrowing effect* of stress.

The narrowing effect of stress works like this. When stress has a hold of you, your attention begins to narrow and hyperfocus. This is your brain's way of attempting to drill down to the problem at hand to try to fix it. Sometimes this can serve you well, such as when you feel a sudden increase of tension as the congested traffic on the highway moves down to one lane and there is construction on either side. Your attention narrows closely to the road, centering your vehicle, keeping a lookout for construction workers, and attending to the proximity of the car in front of you. The narrowing effect of stress has worked to your advantage in that situation.

But if you are about to give a work presentation and feel your stress and anxiety elevating, the narrowing effect of stress might not be so helpful. You might narrow your focus to one person in the audience you think will be critical of you. Or you might narrow your thoughts to feeling that you aren't prepared or that you will make a mistake. Whatever you have narrowed your attention to, you have limited yourself to. In this case, your stress is doing you a disservice.

In Mike's case, after several weeks of depression and withdrawal, he started to reflect on his behavior and gain some insights about himself. He realized he was not participating in his health or his healing. He was not taking any action to help himself. This was obvious to others, but Mike had been too lost in his thoughts to see it. One day, Mike thought, *I'm a hypocrite. I used to be so open to new possibilities, improving myself, and doing new and interesting things for my family. And now something goes wrong, and I do the opposite and close off.* It was then that Mike realized, *This is not me. I'm someone who improves on things. Thanks to challenges and pressures, I've grown my whole life—with my job and with my parenting. I can do the same with my health. This cancer can be an opportunity for me. This stress will make me better.*

His mind-set was shifting. Although the same challenges remained for Mike, he slowly returned to his previous health habits, social connections, and activities. His confidence grew. His unique stressor became his opportunity—it was a chance to become stronger. He began to look at his lung cancer as a catalyst for change and a personal reminder of the value of his relationships. He began to challenge himself in new ways. He forged new friendships with his neighbors, and he revitalized connections with relatives with whom he'd lost touch. He and his family started to travel and explore places they'd never seen. He took up coaching his son's basketball team for the first time. And even though the demands of his job would likely be too great during his treatment, Mike realized he didn't want to quit working. So after discussions with his boss, he shifted to a part-time consulting role that would allow him to stay connected to the company and contribute his skill set to the younger employees.

What happened here is that Mike brought his character strengths to the forefront. The natural curiosity and openness he'd always had paved a pathway for him to stay open to the new opportunities his stress brought forth. Much of this centered on relationship building. When his cancer treatment started, he turned it into an opportunity to use his curiosity to meet new people also undergoing treatment. He used his self-regulation strength to stick to a disciplined health routine, and he used social intelligence and love to connect with the many people in his life.

The last time I met with Mike, he was doing well. I would actually describe him as thriving, meaning that he was physically and mentally strong and was taking advantage of new opportunities while adeptly handling adversities that arose. He remained committed to his mind-set that his stress was going to continue to help him all the way to the end of his life. This shift in his beliefs about stressors marked a turning point for him. In my observation, it was one of the most important elements of "reclaiming his life," so he could live in ways that were fulfilling.

When it comes to life stressors, many people do not reach the insights or conclusions that Mike did. But it's a perspective that can be learned, and our strengths play a big role in that. Mike learned to use his strength of perspective to keep his eyes on the bigger picture of stress, the reality that stress has the potential to help him or harm him and that he holds the key to that decision. Would he learn to wield stress to his advantage, or would he crumble under the weight of it?

Let's break down what I'm calling the "positivity of stress" into two levels: *eustress* and *motivating distress*.

Eustress

In the mid-twentieth century, Hungarian endocrinologist Hans Selye coined the term "eustress" to refer to good or positive stress—something that causes some upset, concern, or worry, but is ultimately a positive situation or positive stressor. Examples include preparing for your child's birthday party, going on a family vacation, retirement, moving into a new home, or getting promoted at work.

Consider some areas of your life that you know are positive and enjoyable but also cause some stress for you. List a few here:

_____

_____

_____

Do you see the positives in these events? Or do you tend to allow the positives to be boxed out by the related pressures? Explain:

_____

_____

_____

Motivating Distress

This second category of positive stress turns our distress (negative stressors) into useful, beneficial, or meaningful stress. This means that any worry, conflict, or problem you have can also become an opportunity to learn, motivate yourself, improve yourself, or help others. Motivating distress may not take away the worry, but it offers another, equally true perspective: that when one door closes, another is being opened. For example, being rejected for the promotion you expected (door closed) can be an excuse to work even harder or to take a different, more creative approach to your work (door opening). A stressful hospitalization might compel you to take stronger, decisive action to improve your health. Poor treatment by a family member might motivate you to not do the same thing to your own children. A marital separation might lead you to new personal reflections and a fresh look at your relationship.

Growing amid stress is a continuous process. It's like a dialogue we have with ourselves that doesn't have an end. The content of the dialogue is to continually challenge ourselves toward growth and actualizing our life's best potential. If we too often settle into a comfort zone, our growth is stunted, and this ultimately leaves us coming up short of making the most of the life we are given. Without stress, our minds don't stretch and advance. Our knowledge and intellect flatline. Without stress in our relationships, they don't evolve and deepen. Instead, we stagnate and sputter.

Consider these examples that reflect an approach of growing over sputtering:

- Kelly is content with her job but has decided to take evening classes in coaching for use on the job in the future, rather than getting caught up in doing the "same ol' thing" at work.

- Dave was becoming more argumentative in his intimate relationship, which was leading to more stress and verbal fights, so he decided to use this as an opportunity to learn. He picked up two books on building relationships at the bookstore.

- Dominic was experiencing some bullying at school. In addition to reporting the perpetrators, he used these incidents as a catalyst for connecting with any other student he saw being teased or isolated. He did his best to befriend each of these classmates.

- Charlotte went to the doctor's office, where it was determined that she was overweight. Rather than chalking this news up to her family genes and continuing on her same dietary path, she saw this stressor as a chance to motivate herself. She started training for a half marathon and increased her daily intake of fruits and vegetables.

When have you experienced motivating distress? Write down as many examples as you can:

_____

_____

_____

What doors were opened by these challenges?

_____

_____

_____

Let's consider another form of stress, one that goes beyond stressful sputtering and is a direct experience of stress: failure. It is commonplace to feel miserable and upset when we fail at something that is important to us, like not making the basketball team, being fired from your job, or breaking up with your boyfriend or girlfriend. It's normal to feel stressed, sad, and disappointed in these situations. If you then get upset about the stress itself, you'll feel worse. It can be a challenge to admit the struggle and then use optimism to look for the growth, the opportunity, or the long-term benefit in the situation.

But when you do turn failures and stress into growth, there are positive changes that typically occur. In *The Upside of Stress*, scientist Kelly McGonigal reviews a massive amount of stress research and points out that "the most common effects of stress include strengths, growth, and resilience" (McGonigal 2015, 45). She breaks these down into the five most commonly reported positive changes that people experience following a loss, trauma, or life challenge:

1. A sense of personal strength

2. Increased appreciation for life

3. Spiritual growth

4. Enhanced social connections and relationships with others

5. Identifying new possibilities and life directions

TURNING STRESS INTO GROWTH

Review McGonigal's list of five positive changes more closely. Each one is easy to overlook, especially when our attention narrows.

Identify a time when you fell short in a relationship, on a project, for a tryout, a potential award or promotion, or something else important to you. Use your strength of honesty to put detailed words to your experience as you describe it. What happened? How did you respond?

_____

_____

_____

Now consider the situation from a positive/growth angle. What did you learn from this experience? How did it help you in some way? As you answer, be sure to consider each of the five types of positive change that often result from stress.

_____

_____

_____

You have now begun the process of changing your mind-set about stress. I hope you are beginning to notice something important about stress that is usually not clear when stress hits you: it provides you with an opportunity to learn, to challenge yourself, and to become stronger. Now let's take a look at stress from the vantage point of your well-being.

Assess Your Levels of Well-Being

Stress and feeling good are not mutually exclusive. In fact, when we use stress to help us learn and grow, it becomes central to the experience of well-being. Therefore, in order to embrace the positive side of stress, it is necessary to understand well-being.

Well-being is more than feeling happy or content in life. Ancient Greek philosophers conceived of happiness as addressing two main areas: *hedonia* and *eudaimonia*. Hedonia—or hedonism—means to pursue pleasure and avoid pain. We all want to do that! More specifically, it refers to the pleasures you seek in your daily life. You get pleasure from slowly chewing on a bar of chocolate or feeling the crisp wind against your cheeks. Eudaimonia refers to the happiness that comes from life fulfillment, engagement, and meaning. You experience this during a stimulating conversation with a friend or by being busy and productive doing work you love. Both types of happiness are important.

Modern-day psychologists have expanded these early thoughts on happiness into a more comprehensive theory of well-being. One pioneer in this area is theorist and positive psychology founder Martin Seligman (2011), who describes five core areas of well-being:

1. Positive emotions

2. Engagement

3. Relationships (positive)

4. Meaning

5. Accomplishment

These areas are captured by the acronym PERMA. Since Seligman's theory came out, there have been many leaders in the field of positive psychology who have argued for a sixth domain of well-being: health. Since I agree that health is an additional, crucial element in the arena of stress and well-being, I'll present the PERMA-H theory in the following chart:

Area of Well-Being	Description	Example
Positive emotions	Feeling pleasurable emotions such as joy, excitement, interest, and peace.	Although they felt stressed and scared, Daniella and Sophia felt the tingling of excitement in their stomachs as they stood in line for the roller coaster.
Engagement	Absorbing yourself in the task at hand.	Julie was fully engaged in the letter of gratitude she was typing to her mother.
Relationships (positive)	Creating and connecting in healthy relationships that enrich your life.	Steve is very connected to his sister. They spend time together on the weekends and regularly share their weekly stressors and joys.
Meaning	Pursuing or experiencing a sense of connection and purpose that goes beyond yourself (with another person, an institution, or the larger universe).	Jeanne experienced a sense of meaning when she took a walk in the forest and felt a connection with "life" in general.
Accomplishment	Reaching your goals; finding success through benchmarks, awards, or achievements in one or more domains of your life.	Jerry received a job promotion that he'd pursued through seven years of dedication and commitment to hard work.
Health	Experiencing physical health and wellness that feels good in the body and mind. Health is more than simply "the absence of disease"; it is a feeling of vitality regardless of whether or not you are disease-free.	Danny has generally good health habits but feels especially vital and "alive" when he is playing softball with his friends.

Seligman finalized his PERMA theory by highlighting the most important part: the 24 character strengths underpin or serve as pathways to each area of well-being. Whereas any of the character strengths can conceivably serve as a route to any of the PERMA areas, some will be more dominant. For example, perseverance and self-regulation are particularly central for the accomplishment area, while gratitude and spirituality, among other things, are particularly important for the meaning area (Wagner et al. 2018).

Furthermore, there is overlap between each of the areas. For instance, in order to reach any achievement in life, you need to do work or training that's at least somewhat engaging; and no doubt in your positive relationships, you experience plenty of meaning as well as positive emotions. Despite the connections among all these domains of well-being, each stands alone as a unique area that can be independently measured and improved upon.

That is where I invite you to turn your attention now—to an opportunity to develop insights on your own PERMA-H levels.

The questions that follow (which were found to be accurate measurements of the core areas of well-being in a large-scale study by the VIA Institute on Character) are not meant to serve as a comprehensive assessment of each area, but they will give you a first impression of your overall well-being. There are no "good or bad" or "high or low" cutoff scores, as the point here is not to compare yourself to others. The point is to give you a sense of the areas in which you are particularly strong and the areas in which growth is needed.

Let's explore each of the six areas one by one. An example is offered before each set of questions, then you'll be asked to reflect more deeply on your own experience in each domain. For each of the three statements that apply to each area, assign yourself an initial score, considering your life as a whole, using the following rating scale:

5 = Very much like me

4 = Like me

3 = Neither like me nor unlike me

2 = Unlike me

1 = Very much unlike me

Positive Emotions

Example: Joselyn likes to laugh a lot. It seems like there are few situations in which she is not laughing and having a good time. She prioritizes hanging out with her friends three to four times a week, and they go out to bars, restaurants, and local events—talking, hanging out, and just having fun. When she's having fun, she experiences a full range of positive emotions, including joy, interest, love, gratitude, excitement, amusement, desire, and even peacefulness. Joselyn scored high in the area of positive emotions.

_____   I experience pleasure and positive emotions much more than not.

_____   When it comes to physical pleasures in my life, I try to savor them fully.

_____   I often get pleasure from reflecting on the past or imagining good things in the future.

_____   Your total score for positive emotions

When are you most likely to experience positive emotions in your daily life (work, home, school, social, community)? In what specific situations do you feel positive emotions most substantially (such as when you're with your best friend at your favorite restaurant; when you're watching funny videos online)?

_____

_____

_____

_____

How do you use positive emotions to handle your stress?

_____

_____

_____

_____

How important is this area of well-being to you? Is this an area you'd like to improve upon? How might you start? Explore your responses here:

_____

_____

_____

_____

Engagement

Example: Bob can quickly list many examples in his daily life of when he feels like he's "in the zone," or in a state of flow. His favorite is when he's playing tennis and finds his rhythm as he maneuvers on the court. He gets to a point where he's not thinking about each shot, he's just focusing on the game and letting his body take action. Bob also reports being in the zone quite a bit at work, absorbed in team meetings or in one-on-one discussions with colleagues, as well as in crunching numbers on his computer. When he goes home, he fully commits to playing with his five-year-old son, creating make-believe games and following his son's every move and word. Bob scored high on engagement.

_____ Many experiences in my life challenge me and capture my full attention.

_____ My life is full of activities that engage my strengths and connect with who I am as a person.

_____ I often go through the day without much distraction or disengagement.

_____ Your total score for engagement

When are you most likely to be engaged in your daily life (work, home, school, social, community)? In what specific situations do you feel that sense of engagement most substantially (such as when you're writing a poem; when you're talking about the community with your neighbor)?

_____

_____

_____

_____

How do you use engagement to handle your stress?

_____

_____

_____

_____

How important is this area of well-being to you? Is this an area you'd like to improve upon? How might you start? Explore your responses here:

_____

_____

_____

_____

Relationships (Positive)

Example: Sue always seems to focus her attention on other people. She is quick to lend her ear to listen to someone's troubles or her hand to give her time to someone in need. She devotes most of her energy to her children and their friends, offering to support each person. Her neighbors, relatives, and coworkers view her as highly trustworthy and genuine. People can quickly size Sue up to see where she stands on an issue or a situation—and if the situation calls for helping another person, you can bet that's the side she'll be on. Sue scored high in the domain of positive relationships.

_____ I have at least one warm and caring relationship based on mutual giving and receiving.

_____ In times of need, there is someone I can turn to for support.

_____ I feel well loved.

_____ Your total score for positive relationships

When are you most likely to connect through positive relationships in your daily life (work, home, school, social, community)? In what specific situations do you experience positive relationships most substantially (such as when you and your partner are discussing a stressful experience; when you and your coworker are getting lunch and discussing work situations)?

_____

_____

_____

_____

How do your positive relationships help you handle stress?

_____

_____

_____

_____

How important is this area of well-being to you? Is this an area you'd like to improve upon? How might you start? Explore your responses here:

_____

_____

_____

_____

Meaning

Example: Joe is a retired professor who volunteers regularly in his community. He serves as a cook for his neighborhood community center, and he serves on a committee that cleans up local parks. He attends local government meetings and offers his perspective on what would best serve the most people. He feels a sense of purpose every time he participates in these groups. He attends a range of religious and spiritual meetings, ethical forums, churches, and centers, trying to learn as much as he can and attempting to find common ground across groups of people. This gives him a deep sense of connectedness in the world. Joe scored high in the area of meaning.

_____ Most of what I do in my life makes a positive difference in the lives of others.

_____ Most activities that I do in my life give me a sense of purpose and meaning.

_____ I often feel a sense of significance and purpose in my life.

_____ Your total score for meaning

When are you most likely to experience meaning in your daily life (work, home, school, social, community)? In what specific situations do you feel a sense of meaning most substantially (such as when you're watching your adolescent son perform on the debate team at school; when you're practicing meditation or yoga with a group of people)?

_____

_____

_____

_____

How does meaning help you handle your stress? Or how *might* meaning help you manage stress?

_____

_____

_____

_____

How important is this area of well-being to you? Is this an area you'd like to improve upon? How might you start? Explore your responses here:

_____

_____

_____

_____

Accomplishment

Example: Gloria is often described as a go-getter with a type A personality. She has a graduate degree and works hard at everything she does—her relationships, her job, and her recreation activities. She loves setting yearly, weekly, and sometimes even daily goals, and she strives to reach them. Gloria has received special perks at her job for her extra work and for going the extra mile. Over the years, she has received awards and commendations for both her achievements at work and in her community. Gloria scored high on accomplishment.

_____   I give myself enough time to make progress on accomplishing my goals.

_____   I achieve the most important goals I set for myself.

_____   I push myself to get things done and handle my responsibilities.

_____   Your total score for accomplishment

When are you most likely to feel a sense of accomplishment in your daily life (work, home, school, social, community)? In what specific situations do you tap into this domain of well-being most substantially (such as when you reach your goal of responding to a certain number of emails in an hour; when your boss lets you know you did a good job; when you and your partner share your stressors and support each other)?

_____

_____

_____

_____

How does accomplishing your goals help you handle your stress?

_____

_____

_____

_____

How important is this area of well-being to you? Is this an area you'd like to improve upon? How might you start? Explore your responses here:

_____

_____

_____

_____

Health

Example: Alex is in good physical shape, with his body mass index score in the normal range for his age and gender. He walks for twenty minutes a few times a week with his girl-friend. He complements that activity with jogging, swimming, or cycling each week. He eats seven or more servings of fruits and vegetables every day and manages his intake of sugar, fast food, and unhealthy snacks, although he allows himself the occasional indulgence (about once per week). He practices a relaxation or meditation technique each day and makes sure he socializes with friends at least once per week. He doesn't smoke, is a social drinker, and never experiments with drugs. Alex reliably gets seven to nine hours of sleep every night and generally sleeps through the night, getting up only once to use the bathroom. Alex scored high in the domain of health.

_____ Compared to others of the same sex and age, my health is good.

_____ I am satisfied with my current level of health.

_____ My diet, exercise, and sleep habits are healthy.

_____ Your total score for health

In what areas of your life do you feel most "alive" and vital (work, home, school, social, community)? Describe your experience of "health" in those areas:

_____

_____

_____

_____

How does your good health or lack of good health impact how you handle stress?

_____

_____

_____

_____

How important is this area of well-being to you? Is this an area you'd like to improve upon? How might you start? Are there certain health habits (sleeping, eating, exercising) that you want to target? Explore your responses here:

_____

_____

_____

_____

By answering these questions, you now have a good idea of your well-being in the six key areas. You can see the areas you are strong in, which will be important resources for you in managing stress. Those areas that might be less developed can be tapped into with your strengths. Keeping these well-being areas in mind will help you as we proceed along in this workbook.

Identify Goals to Guide Your Efforts

You have explored your stress levels and your well-being levels, and you have a good idea of where you are now. Your answers to questionnaires can point to areas where you might want to grow. Think about what you want most in your life at this moment in time. There are many possible pursuits, such as creating more happiness, adding more stress management tools, building more confidence, finding a lasting relationship, improving your health, or advancing in your job or career. Considering this will help you set an initial goal for your journey toward stress relief.

Get specific and look to the work you did in this chapter. What is one course of action you can start with? Can you tackle one of the stressors you identified earlier in the chapter? Can you enhance one of the six areas of well-being that could use improvement? Maybe you can experiment with applying the "stress is helpful" mind-set to one of your life stressors?

Explore your initial goal here:

_____

_____

_____

_____

Learn. Practice. SHARE.

In this chapter, you've learned about the positivity of stress. You took stock of your current stress and well-being levels and began to reflect more deeply on how these play out in your life.

An important way to continue your growth is to connect with others about your learnings and applications. Consider this: What is the most important insight or activity for you to share with others right now?

Before moving on to chapter 2, share an insight, practice, or goal with at least one person. You might explain the "stress is helpful" mind-set to a loved one today or share an insight on the positivity of stress on social media. Or you could ask a friend about one of their areas of well-being. Explore your "share" below and note with whom you will connect:

_____

_____

_____

_____

CHAPTER 2

Assess Your Strengths

Mary is a thirty-five-year-old, working part-time as a department store clerk and an aspiring writer. Having grown up in a large family, she often felt overlooked by her brothers and parents. She is now married with a two-year-old boy. Mary is interested in getting to know herself better. She likes taking tests online, reading popular books and magazines, and surfing websites and blogs that offer strategies on parenting, health, pottery, and tai chi. She had been experiencing writer's block for the last year, only able to put out an occasional short blog article but nothing substantive. She did not feel much meaning in her work at the department store, but she enjoyed the steady paycheck. What was particularly bothersome to Mary was the rising tensions she was feeling of parenting a young child. Her son's colic was followed by frequent ear infections, then a medical scare that turned out to be a minor heart defect. The stress had taken a toll on her relationship with her husband, and if it weren't for their child, she figured their short periods of separation for two to three days might have turned into a divorce.

Mary was seeking more in her professional life, so she submitted a few job applications and starting prepping for interviews. She was having coffee with a friend one day who said to her, "They'll ask about your strengths, Mary. What are they?" Normally, Mary had a lot to say about a lot of topics, but to this question, she went blank. She looked away, feeling a bit of uneasiness in her stomach. This was a standard question asked at interviews, but Mary didn't know how to respond. To say, "I'm good at writing" or "I like to create bowls using clay" sounded positive, but like statements that didn't do justice to the question. Mary knew there was a better way to describe her best qualities, but she felt unsure of herself.

It turns out that Mary's highest character strengths are curiosity, kindness, gratitude, and judgment. *Can this be true?* she wondered as she reviewed the results of the survey she'd just taken. *Well, those do seem pretty accurate. I am always exploring new topics online, and I do go out of my way to help people. I'm a good critical thinker, and I always seem to be grateful for even the little things in life.*

For Mary, it felt like she was going from black and white to color. A veil had been lifted, and she was seeing herself with greater clarity—more vividly. She began to apply her strengths to the areas of her life that were stressful, curiously exploring how to be kinder to shoppers at the department store and also to her husband and son. She began writing down all the moments she felt thankful for to emphasize them. As a result of embracing her strengths, her stress began to morph into greater positivity and feelings of well-being.

Moving in the Direction of Strengths

Mary, like all of us, has her own unique profile of character strengths. The VIA Classification of character strengths is a way of making that uniqueness more concrete and apparent. It's a description, not a prescription. In other words, it describes core parts of a person's character, or personality, but it does not prescribe precisely what that person needs to do with them in their life. Mary is particularly strong in gratitude and kindness, while other people are especially humble and creative or brave and hopeful. In fact, given the 24 character strengths that make up a person's individualized profile, there are over 600 sextillion possible combinations (that's 23 zeroes after the number 6!).

No two people are the same. Not only that, but each person has a different way of expressing each strength. Love might be expressed through thoughtful acts, compassionate listening, well-spent time with someone, affirming words, or nurturing touch. Humor might be expressed through jokes, laughter and smiling, clever wit, goofy behavior, or comic storytelling. We all have a different way of experiencing and expressing our character strengths.

This chapter will focus on awareness and use of your strengths. To cultivate awareness, you'll assess and explore several categories of strengths that reside within you, then you'll assess and explore how you use them—that is, whether you are bringing your strengths into as much action in your life as you could be.

All 24 Strengths Matter

A decade ago, I was giving an extended workshop on character strengths and speaking with the group about how all 24 of them were important. One of the attendees raised her hand. When I called on her, she stood up and exclaimed with excitement, "These strengths are like Starbucks coffee sizes."

"How so?" I asked with genuine curiosity.

"Well, Starbucks only serves large sizes—Tall, Grande, and Venti. And that's the way our character strengths are. They are all big and important in our lives!"

"That's true," I said with a laugh. Then, building off her metaphor, "Our signature strengths are the biggest of all—the Ventis. Our middle strengths are the Grandes. And our lesser strengths are the Talls—still big and important."

This woman's insight was, of course, correct. She had quickly caught on to the reality that, in our daily life, there is no small or unimportant strength among this group of 24. These strengths are all "large" in our lives, our relationships, our health, our goals, and our future potential.

While research studies show that perseverance is a particularly important strength for achieving goals, it might be that you tap into your "Venti strengths" of creativity and love of learning to come up with interesting goals and carry them out. And research may point out that gratitude is an important strength for creating life meaning, but you might find the greatest meaning through your Venti strengths of expressing kindness and fairness to others. Therefore, it becomes particularly important for each of us to understand our own unique profile of strengths. What are your Ventis, Grandes, and Talls?

Understanding Your Strengths Profile

The first step is to figure out your own character strengths profile—your full rank order of character strengths from 1 to 24. You can generate your profile at http://www.viacharacter .org/www, where over seven million people have taken the VIA Survey. The survey is free and you'll receive immediate rank-order results. In fact, there's nothing else like it out there. It is the gold-standard test that scientists and practitioners recommend for assessing character strengths. After you review your results, you'll have the option to purchase a personalized report, but that is *not* required for this workbook. At this point, simply print out your results and keep them handy as you engage with this chapter (and with the rest of this book). When you look at your profile, you'll immediately see those strengths that come up highest, lowest, and in the middle of your profile.

To understand your character strengths profile, it is useful to understand the various *types* of character strengths that you have. Here's a snapshot of the types we'll be exploring, along with some examples of each, so you can see where we are heading. This chapter will focus on the first four types, as those have the strongest conceptual or research support (Niemiec 2018).

Type of Character Strength	Definition	Example
Signature strengths	Your highest strengths; these are most central to who you are and best capture your uniqueness. They show up across many situations and are most energizing and easiest for you to use.	Carol turned to her highest strength of perseverance to pull an all-nighter and finish her work project before the meeting.
Happiness strengths	Strengths that have the strongest connection to happiness, according to different research groups around the world. These are zest, hope, love, gratitude, and curiosity.	Rick felt stressed and overwhelmed by a challenging day at work but quickly turned to his strength of gratitude to see the positive in his situation and feel grateful that he has a good job and that he can meaningfully contribute to others' lives. This gave him a happiness boost for the rest of the evening.
Lower strengths	These are your lowest strengths of the 24, likely those you have not put much effort into deeply understanding or developing.	Despite prudence being her lowest strength, Maggie applied it to carefully plan out a schedule for her daughter's birthday party. She turned a stressful situation into a fun and successful event.
Phasic strengths	These are situational strengths you bring forth strongly when the situation demands it.	As tension mounted during a conversation that turned "political" at a family gathering, Daryl used kindness to compassionately listen to others' viewpoints and make thoughtful remarks to each person before he changed the subject.
Supportive strengths	Strengths that aren't especially high or low for you; they may support or enhance your other strengths.	At the team meeting, Rosita's midlevel strength of zest emerged as she exerted energy and enthusiasm that helped her maintain her signature strength of leadership.

Lost strengths	Those strengths that have gone dormant due to your lack of awareness or use of them over a period of time.	Aaron's strength of curiosity had been actively discouraged by his family while growing up ("Aaron, don't ask questions!"), so he hasn't given it much attention in his young adulthood.

Signature Strengths: Your Best Self

Let's start with arguably the most important category: the top strengths in your profile. These are the strengths that relate most to who you are as a person. Just as your handwritten signature on a piece of paper is unique to you, so are your signature strengths. Most people have around five signature strengths, although that does not necessarily apply to everyone. Some have more, some have less.

A good way to describe signature strengths is that they are very likely to involve the "three E's" (Niemiec 2018):

- *Essential:* The strengths are core to who you are. For example, Monica describes her spirituality as being "central to me. It's at the core of who I am and how I operate in the world. I try to be a reflection of my beliefs and faith."

- *Energizing:* The strengths are uplifting and give you a boost of energy or joy. J. P. points out he gets a small energy burst each time he asks someone a question. "That's my curiosity coming out. It makes me happy when I use it."

- *Effortless:* The strengths come easy and natural to you—you can use them without effort. Zara, for instance, explains that being honest is almost never challenging. "Honesty seeps from my pores. I don't even think about it, I just default on being honest with people, even when it's difficult sometimes."

Your signature strengths are important, not only as qualities that describe your identity, but also as pathways to various outcomes, such as greater happiness. Studies consistently show that the regular use of signature strengths leads people to lower depression levels and higher happiness levels (Gander et al. 2013; Seligman et al. 2005). We'll discuss this later when we focus on strengths use. For now, let's stick to strengths awareness.

One way to discover your signature strengths is to formally assess them with the Signature Strengths Survey. Similar to yet different from the VIA Survey mentioned earlier (see the website link above), this simple, two-step scientific test was created and validated by the VIA Institute on Character.

Signature Strengths Survey

Step 1. Read the following descriptions of the 24 character strengths. Everyone uses these strengths at times. Put a check in the box next to those strengths that are *absolutely essential* to you, that define *who you are as a person,* that are *part of who you are.* For example, someone who has devoted his life to helping others might choose kindness as one of his essential strengths; someone who prides herself on being able to figure out other people might consider social intelligence key to who she is; and someone who is constantly seeking out new information might consider love of learning to be essential. Most people check just a few essential strengths. Please describe *the person you are,* NOT the person you wish you could be. Also, think about your life *in general,* not how you've behaved in only one or two situations.

Essential Strength?	Character Strengths
	1. Creativity: You are viewed as a creative person; you see, do, and/or create things that are of use; you think of unique ways to solve problems and be productive.
	2. Curiosity: You are an explorer; you seek novelty; you are interested in new activities, ideas, and people; you are open to new experiences.
	3. Judgment/Critical Thinking: You are analytical; you examine things from all sides; you do not jump to conclusions, but instead attempt to weigh all the evidence when making decisions.
	4. Love of Learning: You often find ways to deepen your knowledge and experiences; you regularly look for new opportunities to learn; you are passionate about building knowledge.
	5. Perspective: You take the "big picture" view of things; others turn to you for wise advice; you help others make sense of the world; you learn from your mistakes.
	6. Bravery/Courage: You face your fears and overcome challenges and adversity; you stand up for what is right; you do not shrink in the face of pain or inner tension or turmoil.
	7. Perseverance: You keep going and going when you have a goal in mind; you attempt to overcome all obstacles; you finish what you start.
	8. Honesty: You are a person of high integrity and authenticity; you tell the truth, even when it hurts; you present yourself to others in a sincere way; you take responsibility for your actions.

Essential Strength?	Character Strengths
	9. Zest: You are enthusiastic toward life; you are highly energetic and activated; you use your energy to the fullest degree.
	10. Love: You are warm and genuine to others; you not only share but are open to receiving love from others; you value growing close and intimate with others.
	11. Kindness: You do good things for people; you help and care for others; you are generous and giving; you are compassionate.
	12. Social Intelligence: You pay close attention to social nuances and the emotions of others; you have good insight into what makes people "tick"; you seem to know what to say and do in any social situation.
	13. Teamwork: You are a collaborative and participative member of groups and teams; you are loyal to your group; you feel a strong sense of duty to your group; you always do your share.
	14. Fairness: You believe strongly in an equal and just opportunity for all; you don't let personal feelings bias your decisions about others; you treat people the way you want to be treated.
	15. Leadership: You positively influence those you lead; you prefer to lead than to follow; you are very good at organizing and taking charge for the collective benefit of the group.
	16. Forgiveness: You readily let go of hurt after you are wronged; you give people a second chance; you are not vengeful or resentful; you accept people's shortcomings.
	17. Humility: You let your accomplishments speak for themselves; you see your own goodness but prefer to focus the attention on others; you do not see yourself as more special than others; you admit your imperfections.
	18. Prudence: You are wisely cautious; you are planful and conscientious; you are careful to not take undue risks or do things you might later regret.
	19. Self-Regulation: You are a very disciplined person; you manage your vices and bad habits; you stay calm and cool under pressure; you manage your impulses and emotions.

Essential Strength?	Character Strengths
	20. Appreciation of Beauty & Excellence: You notice the beauty and excellence around you; you are often awestruck by beauty, greatness, and the moral goodness you witness; you are often filled with wonder.
	21. Gratitude: You regularly experience and express thankfulness; you don't take the good things that happen in your life for granted; you tend to feel blessed in many circumstances.
	22. Hope: You are optimistic, expecting the best to happen; you believe in and work toward a positive future; you can think of many pathways to reach your goals.
	23. Humor: You are playful; you love to make people smile and laugh; your sense of humor helps you connect closely to others; you brighten gloomy situations with fun and jokes.
	24. Spirituality: Your life is infused with a sense of meaning and purpose; you feel a connection with something larger than yourself; your faith informs who you are and your place in the universe; you maintain a regular spiritual/religious practice.
	None of these characteristics is more essential to who I am than any of the others. Remember, you should choose this option if the strengths are all equally essential to you, NOT because you think they should be equally essential.

Step 2. Review the strengths you checked. Do any of these strengths stand out as more important to who you are than the others? If so, put a second check in the box next to those strengths.

This Signature Strengths Survey and the online VIA Survey, while centered on the same 24 strengths, use different methods for arriving at the results. This means that you might not generate identical results from each assessment. Therefore, taking the approach outlined in the next section is important as you reflect on and explore your unique signature.

Confirming Your Signature

Now that you've identified your signature strengths, it's time to examine how these strengths *fit* you. The questions below are intended to help you understand the importance of each strength in your life and see the potency of each one in the person you've become today.

To start, compare your top five strengths from the Signature Strengths Survey with the top five strengths identified by the VIA Survey. Are they the same? If so, complete the questions for each below, making sure to include those for which you made two checkmarks. If not, to cover all your top strengths in each survey, feel free to go beyond the space allotted for your top five to explore those as well.

Character strength #1: _____

In what ways is this strength a true description of you? Of how you operate in the world?

_____

_____

_____

How has this strength shown up most in your life? How has it helped you most? Be sure to consider your family, work, relationships, school, health, leisure pursuits, social life, spiritual life, and community.

_____

_____

_____

Character strength #2: _____

In what ways is this strength a true description of you? Of how you operate in the world?

_____

_____

_____

How has this strength shown up most in your life? How has it helped you most? Be sure to consider your family, work, relationships, school, health, leisure pursuits, social life, spiritual life, and community.

_____

_____

_____

Character strength #3: _____

In what ways is this strength a true description of you? Of how you operate in the world?

_____

_____

_____

How has this strength shown up most in your life? How has it helped you most? Be sure to consider your family, work, relationships, school, health, leisure pursuits, social life, spiritual life, and community.

_____

_____

_____

Character strength #4: _____

In what ways is this strength a true description of you? Of how you operate in the world?

_____

_____

_____

How has this strength shown up most in your life? How has it helped you most? Be sure to consider your family, work, relationships, school, health, leisure pursuits, social life, spiritual life, and community.

_____

_____

_____

Character strength #5: _____

In what ways is this strength a true description of you? Of how you operate in the world?

_____

_____

_____

How has this strength shown up most in your life? How has it helped you most? Be sure to consider your family, work, relationships, school, health, leisure pursuits, social life, spiritual life, and community.

_____

_____

_____

With your signature strengths at hand, you are building a solid foundation of self-awareness, understanding many of the ways they show up in your life. Let's look at another way strengths can connect you to happiness.

Happiness Strengths: Another Path to Feeling Good

The majority of us, whether we admit it or not, want happiness. A survey of ten thousand people from forty-eight countries found that happiness was more important to them than success, intelligence, knowledge, maturity, wisdom, relationships, wealth, or meaning in life (Oishi, Diener, and Lucas 2007). The good news is that character strengths seem to go along with happiness like your foot gliding into a cozy shoe.

Study after study—across different groups of people—began to show that five character strengths are most aligned with happiness, even *causing* happiness (Buschor, Proyer, and Ruch 2013; Park, Peterson, and Seligman 2004; Proyer, Ruch, and Buschor 2013). There's now been enough attention paid to these five strengths that some researchers have dubbed them "the happiness strengths":

- Zest—feeling energetic and full of vitality

- Hope—feeling optimistic and focused on the future

- Love—feeling warm and being closely connected to others

- Gratitude—feeling appreciative and expressing thanks regularly

- Curiosity—feeling interested and wanting to explore new topics and situations

These happiness strengths, all of which reside in you, serve as another pathway for you to build your happiness. Let's examine them, one by one.

Exploring Zest

What number is zest in your rank-order profile of strengths on the VIA Survey? _____

When do you feel most energetic and zestful?

_____

_____

_____

Name a situation in which you used zest. How did zest help you in that situation?

_____

_____

_____

_____

Exploring Hope

What number is hope in your rank-order profile of strengths on the VIA Survey? _____

When do you feel most hopeful and optimistic?

_____

_____

_____

Name a situation in which you used hope. How did hope help you in that situation?

_____

_____

_____

_____

Exploring Love

What number is love in your rank-order profile of strengths on the VIA Survey? _____

When do you feel most loving and connected to others?

_____

_____

_____

Name a situation in which you used love. How did love help you in that situation?

_____

_____

_____

_____

Exploring Gratitude

What number is gratitude in your rank-order profile of strengths on the VIA Survey? _____

When do you feel most grateful and appreciative during the day?

_____

_____

_____

Name a situation in which you used gratitude. How did gratitude help you in that situation?

_____

_____

_____

_____

Exploring Curiosity

What number is curiosity in your rank-order profile of strengths on the VIA Survey? ____

When do you feel most curious and interested during the day?

_____

_____

_____

Name a situation in which you used curiosity. How did curiosity help you in that situation?

_____

_____

_____

_____

Now let's turn to another category of strengths that has been linked with well-being.

Lower Strengths: Not Weaknesses, Still Strengths

In looking at your VIA Survey results, it is normal (and very tempting) to spend time lamenting or feeling upset by your lower (also called lesser) strengths. And you may automatically judge your lower strengths as your weaknesses. Our negativity bias is always looking for flaws or problems in ourselves. It's only natural to find yourself looking at your lowest strengths and exclaiming, "I don't have any self-regulation!" "I'm not at all creative," or "Being able to forgive others is a big weakness of mine."

Of course, it's possible that these are weaknesses, but that's not the best way to approach this strength category. Here's why: the VIA Survey is a test of strengths, some of which you have more of—it is not a test of your weaknesses, problems, or psychopathology. Since the test is not measuring weaknesses, we cannot come to a conclusion that the test is not offering. To refer to your lesser strengths as weaknesses is to get locked into a deficit-based mind-set, viewing yourself as something "to be corrected" or something that is "flawed" or "wrong." Instead, it's more productive to consider all 24 strengths as your own, with some of them coming forth more forcefully or adeptly within you than others. In regard to your lower strengths, it is possible you have given them less attention over the years or don't value them as much as your other strengths.

All that said, lesser strengths are important, and research has revealed that they provide another way to boost well-being when you focus on them (Proyer et al. 2015; Rust, Diessner, and Reade 2009). Consider the character strengths that are lowest in your VIA Survey profile. Though there's not a magic number of lesser strengths, focus for now on your bottom five. (If you've not yet taken the test online, rank your strengths yourself using either the table of them in the introduction to this book or the table in this chapter.) Which of these strengths do you think least describes who you are? Which are least energizing to you? Which ones would you have to exert substantial effort to bring forth?

Write down three to five of your lower strengths:

_____

_____

_____

_____

_____

How does it feel to call these "lower" strengths? Some people feel disappointed that these strengths appear at the bottom of their profile and wish they were higher up. Others are self-critical and think that they're not being as strong as they could be. Still others are accepting of or content with this grouping when viewed alongside their higher-ranking strengths—it feels accurate to them. What is your reaction?

_____

_____

_____

Pick one of your lower strengths and one domain of your life (work, family, social, community). Describe how you have used that strength, with at least some success, in that domain.

Lower strength: _____

Domain: _____

Past use: _____

Phasic Strengths: When Do You Rise to the Occasion?

As mentioned earlier, our phasic strengths are *nonsignature* strengths that we exhibit when a situation calls for it. We are likely to express our signature strengths strongly in a wide range of situations, but phasic strengths come out only in particular situations. To be a phasic strength, you not only express it in the necessary situation, but you express it strongly. In fact, someone observing you who doesn't know your profile might perceive the phasic strength you are expressing as your unique signature!

The Broadway hit musical *Hamilton* reminds us to "rise up" and take "your shot." Similarly, a phasic strength means we rise up to the occasion. We see a situation present itself in front of us and we take our shot. We bring forward an important part of ourselves.

Imagine you are at a town hall meeting with about a hundred community members present. Several people vocally express an opinion different from your own. Then one woman, who is typically quiet, stands up and expresses the counterpoint argument in a strong yet appropriate way for all to hear. She then asks, "Who's with me?" Twenty hands go up. One of this woman's phasic strengths might be bravery because she's using it strongly when the situation calls for it.

When my wife is away for an evening and I'm alone watching my three young children, my prudence (not a signature strength) emerges. I become highly organized and planful with my kids, and I accomplish the necessary routine tasks for each of them, as well as some additional fun activities, all within a short time frame. In such situations, it appears that prudence rises up to become a phasic strength for me.

How about you? As you reflect on your nonsignature strengths, consider these questions:

- Have you risen to the occasion with strong perseverance when you needed to complete a project?

- Turned to curiosity instead of anxiety when you felt overwhelmed by stress?

- Brought forth significant zest every time you had a presentation to give?

- Displayed exemplary self-regulation/self-control when your child repeatedly disagreed with you?

- When have you risen up?

Write down your observations:

_____

_____

_____

_____

_____

Claiming Your Phasic Strengths

Think of a recent time when you were stressed. Consider your actions and how you approached the situation. What was most effective about how you handled the situation? Perhaps you resolved the situation, managed it, or at least got through it. Take note of the character strength you brought forth the most in this situation. Do you typically bring forth this strength in a clear and strong way at difficult times? If yes, it might be a phasic strength. Explore that possibility here.

Phasic strength: _____

Story of a situation when it showed up: _____

_____

_____

_____

How this phasic strength appears in your life: _____

_____

_____

_____

A Point of Clarification: Other Strengths Matter Too!

We've been exploring your character strengths, both your signature strengths and those that don't show up as strongly in you. But there are, of course, additional elements that go into the unique makeup of every human being.

First, there are many physical qualities that describe us that have nothing to do with our character strengths, such as our height, weight, eye color, hair type, and blood pressure. Then there are personality qualities that are distinct from character strengths, such as our level of neuroticism and our extraversion/introversion level. And then there are other kinds of human strengths different from character strengths, such as our talents/abilities, skills, interests, values, and resources (Niemiec 2018).

To clarify these areas further, review the categories below. As you do so, it's important to understand the connections character strengths have with each area, so examples are provided for each. It is your character strengths that help you activate the other strength categories. In order to get your talent for music or sport to soar, for instance, you need to activate your character strengths of perseverance and self-regulation to devote many hours to disciplined practice and you need to call on your strength of hope to envision the future. And when you connect with any of your external resources, you are likely tapping into your social intelligence, kindness, and fairness, among other character strengths.

Personal Quality	Definition	Examples	Example of How Character Strengths Connect with This Personal Quality
Character Strengths	Central, positive parts of your identity; essential to who you are	Curiosity, bravery, perseverance, honesty, kindness, fairness, forgiveness, self-regulation, hope, humor, gratitude	N/A
Talents/ Abilities	Hardwired, innate abilities; what you naturally do well	Spatial reasoning, logic, mathematical capacity, interpersonal aptitude, musicality, athleticism	Jason developed his talent for running by using his self-regulation to stay disciplined and focused and his prudence to create a regular schedule.
Skills	Proficiencies you can develop; what you train to do	Computer programming, anger management, woodworking, communication	Trina's strength of hope for a better job and a better future propelled her to build as many job skills as she could in such areas as software programs and social media.
Interests	Your passions, hobbies, engaging activities; what you enjoy doing regularly	Cooking, painting, playing sports, crafting, attaining collectibles, writing, reading certain genres, social media, gaming	Billy loves to play video and online games. This is fueled by his curiosity in seeing different characters in the games and his critical thinking, which involves looking analytically at all the detailed ways he could possibly win a game.
Values	Your principles or standards for how you live or wish to live; what you internally hold dear (*does not address your actual behavior*)	Thoughts/feelings relating to having a happy family, achievement, hard work, caring for others, having peaceful conversations	Family values figure most prominently in Anne's life. She puts those values into action with her character strengths—namely, her love, her kindness, and the humility she displays by focusing on her family members above all else.

Resources	Your external supports that help you and sustain you	Supportive family, friends, a safe neighborhood, a spiritual community, a volunteer group	Joan and Chuck wanted to live in a safe, tight-knit neighborhood in a good school district. When they moved, their planning strength of prudence and aspirational strength of hope helped make this positive resource a reality for them.

We'll return to these other categories of strength in the next chapter, when we focus on building up the totality of your strengths resources.

You Have 24 Strength Capacities to Use

Your 24 strengths are "capacities" within you. This means you have the capability to use each one of them. There is always potential within you for expression of your strengths. You use all 24 to some degree each week, and some strengths are used as often as every hour, although you may not be aware of it.

Consider the curiosity you use when you're surfing the web, the self-regulation required for your morning routine of brushing your teeth and getting dressed, your prudence in driving carefully to work. These are examples of strengths use to a very small degree. A larger dose of strengths use occurs when you exert creativity in proposing a new work project to your boss, social intelligence when you listen empathically to your brother's struggles, fairness when you stick up for someone being teased, and spirituality when you sit down to meditate despite urges to skip your practice.

Your character strengths capacities, valued throughout time and history, are all within you.

Assessing Strengths Use

When it comes to working with your character strengths, awareness and understanding are beneficial and will take you far—giving you increased well-being. But it is action with your character strengths that matters most. As the influential writer Goethe said, "Knowing is not enough, we must apply. Willing is not enough, we must do." Using your character strengths offers you that extra boost. So why not use those parts of yourself that are most energizing, easy to use, and most authentic to who you are?

Using your character strengths more in your daily life generates further awareness of yourself and the many situations in which you can apply your strengths. Consider the "virtuous circle" shown below in which one positive leads to another in a potentially ongoing cycle of positivity and goodness.

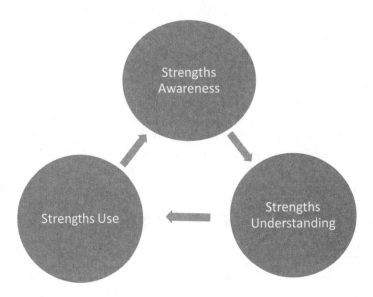

As you become more aware of your strengths, explore them through reflection, and glean insights about them, it is natural to want to begin taking action in different ways. This is what happened to Cecilia, a middle-aged banker, who said this after identifying her character strengths and reflecting on them:

> It feels as though I have doors within myself that are opening up. There are these areas of myself that I had closed off, like my hope, my creativity, and my leadership. I wasn't giving them any attention. And yet these are important parts of myself. I am ready to get back to me. I need to keep these strength doors open!

The next step for Cecilia is to widen her signature strengths use. How about you? Let's take a closer look at how regularly you are *using* your signature strengths.

Signature Strengths Use Test

For the exercise below, there are no right or wrong answers, no specific score to achieve. Instead, use the questions as a tool for self-insight and exploration and for gauging your improvement with strengths use.

Start by listing your signature strengths. This will help you keep them at the top of your mind as you answer each question. List five to seven of your top strengths:

_____   _____

_____   _____

_____   _____

_____   _____

Next, use the following scale to answer these questions about your signature strengths:

1	2	3	4	5	6	7
Strongly Disagree	Moderately Disagree	Slightly Disagree	Neither Agree nor Disagree	Slightly Agree	Moderately Agree	Strongly Agree

_____ I use my signature strengths regularly each day.

_____ I come up with a wide range of ways to use my signature strengths.

_____ I use my signature strengths to manage stress.

_____ Life challenges are not as difficult for me because I use my signature strengths.

_____ I use my signature strengths regularly in my personal and close relationships.

_____ I find ways to use my signature strengths to help or support others.

_____ I often use my signature strengths to help me be productive in my work.

_____ I use several of my signature strengths at work each day.

_____ I am happiest when I am using my signature strengths in my life.

_____ When I use my signature strengths, I feel I am expressing my best self.

_____ Total score for signature strengths use

REFLECTION

Examine your responses more closely. What strikes you most? What is interesting or surprising?

_____

_____

_____

Do you notice any patterns in your responses? All high, midrange, or low scores? One or two questions on which you scored lower? One area (stress questions or relationship questions) in which you scored high?

_____

_____

_____

Make note of anything you would like to explore further, even if it's just targeting one of the questions. For example, you might wish to focus more on how much you use your signature strengths at work.

_____

_____

_____

How Are You Already Using Your Character Strengths?

It is easy to overlook your character strengths use. It can be subtle. We can quickly take each of the 24 strengths for granted. However, they are always there, waiting just below the surface of your attention, ready to be expressed (Niemiec 2014). This is especially evident in our daily routines, which are ripe with potential to learn about our strengths.

Take Kara, for instance, who realized it was her strength of curiosity that was driving her to check what her friends were saying and doing on Facebook. And she loved going on

Instagram as well, because she could express her creativity and her appreciation of beauty in all the photos posted there. Or Jalen, who took note that he used his self-regulation while brushing his teeth for exactly two minutes each morning and his prudence while carefully choosing a healthy and balanced breakfast each day in light of his recent diabetes diagnosis.

Fill in the table below to reflect on ten routine activities you probably do every day or most days during a typical week. See if you can detect one or more of the character strengths you are using during the activity, even if the use is subtle (as modeled in the first example given).

Routine Activity	Character Strength(s) Used	How You Use the Strength(s)
Washing your hair	*Prudence; curiosity*	*I'm careful to thoroughly wash each layer of hair.* *I'm interested and curious about the scent of the shampoo and also about how many hair follicles I have on my head!*
Rising to your alarm clock		
Brushing your teeth		
Driving to work		
Making your lunch		
E-mailing a coworker or friend		

Posting something to social media		
Talking with a family member		
Eating a snack		
Reading a book, magazine, or online article		
Walking around your neighborhood		
Other activity:		

We use our strengths in so many ways, big and small. They are easy to take for granted, easy to overlook, and easy to discount in ourselves and in others. Realizing the fact that our strengths are already all around us is empowering. Look a little closer, and you'll see them. Unleash your potential!

Use a Signature Strength in a New Way

Let's take your strengths use one step further, which science tells us is especially beneficial. Randomized controlled studies show that there is an activity that is particularly good at bolstering happiness and lowering depression: using one of your signature strengths in a new way each day (Gander et al. 2013; Seligman et al. 2005).

The activity is straightforward. Choose one of your highest signature strengths. Then, each day for the next week, use the strength in a novel way, no matter how small. Someone choosing social intelligence might strike up a conversation with someone new on one day and then talk about their emotions with a loved one the next day. Someone choosing curiosity might try a new food one day and ask a colleague a new question the next day.

Make this activity part of your regular strengths practice by downloading this blank worksheet at http://www.newharbinger.com/42808.

Signature strength:	
	How You Used or Will Use This Strength Each Day
Day 1	
Day 2	
Day 3	
Day 4	
Day 5	
Day 6	
Day 7	

Here's another spin on the same type of exercise. Instead of taking one signature strength and using it in a new way each day of the week, take your top seven strengths and apply each one differently on each day of the week. For example, on Monday, I might use my love strength in a new way by spending some extra time to thoughtfully and genuinely listen to a work colleague. On Tuesday, I could use my creativity in a new way by writing a poem; and on Wednesday, I can use my spirituality strength to try out meditation. If you prefer this approach, use the following grid:

Day	Character Strength Used	Description of Use
1		
2		
3		
4		
5		
6		
7		

Using our strengths in new ways can be a fun, challenging, and highly rewarding adventure that increases happiness and well-being.

Learn. Practice. SHARE.

In this chapter, you've learned about the different types of character strengths you have. You've explored your signature strengths, happiness strengths, lower strengths, and phasic strengths, then began to look at your strength use levels. Your practice involved moving from exploration of signature strengths to using them more in your life, especially in new and different ways.

Before moving on from this chapter, consider this: What is most important for you to share with others right now?

Share an insight, practice, or goal with one person. You might share with a friend the concept of phasic strengths and why this is important. You might use one of your signature strengths in a way that helps a loved one. Or you might post one of your responses to any of the questions in this chapter and explain why on social media. Explore your "share" below and note with whom you will connect:

_____

_____

_____

_____

_____

PART ONE

Cultivate a Strengths Mind-Set

CHAPTER 3

Respond to Stress with Your Strengths

I was never very good at math, nor was I especially interested in it. I would avoid math homework for as long as I could, and when I finally got to it, I would suffer through it. Thus, it came as a surprise to me that I would create an equation for how to think about, understand, and manage your stress. This simple equation can help you view your stress in a concrete way:

$$S = P - C$$

(S)tress = (P)ressure minus (C)apacity

Stress refers to the total amount of pressures and demands you are under after you consider your various capacities, resources, and adaptations. Going by this equation, there are only two ways to successfully manage your stress: decrease the pressure you are under or increase your capacity to handle it. Simplistic as this sounds for something as complex as stress, it at least gives us a starting point.

Pressures and capacities are wide-ranging and versatile. To best understand them, we should view them from a biopsychosocial-spiritual perspective. We can have *biological pressures*, such as bodily tension, illness, and disease; *psychological pressures*, such as depression, anxiety, anger, and self-defeating thoughts; *social pressures*, such as isolation, teasing, rejection, neglect, and difficulty relating to people; and *spiritual pressures*, such as experiencing a lack of meaning or life purpose. In addition, each segment of life comes with its own pressures, such as work demands (long hours, taking on extra projects), parenting demands (driving kids to after-school activities, taking care of their basic needs), school demands (homework, studying for exams), family/relationship demands (handling conflicts, feeling unloved by a partner, struggling to make enough time for your relationship), and so on.

Likewise, there are a range of capacities we can engender, such as *biological capacities* (getting an optimal amount of sleep, healthy eating); *psychological capacities* (creating feelings of peace and joy); *social capacities* (spending time with friends); and *spiritual capacities* (doing activities that promote meaning, spending time in nature). Capacities also involve your character strengths and your many other positive qualities, such as your interests, abilities, and resources, all of which will be explored in this chapter.

The goal of this equation is to look at stress and understand it in a different way, not to bring your stress level to zero. The equation is also immediately practical. If your pressure is particularly high or your capacity level especially low, then you'll no doubt experience ongoing stress. But if your capacity is particularly high, then your stress is probably well managed and/or does not occupy much of your attention.

We can look at the equation and make some general interpretations of it in relation to stress. If you have an extreme level of either "pressure" or "capacity," then the descriptions below will likely be spot-on. But even if your levels are more midrange, you can still use these four alternatives as a launching pad for understanding your stress:

$\uparrow$P, $\downarrow$C = **Overwhelmed.** The low capacity and resources for managing the high degree of pressure you are under is the perfect recipe for distress.

$\downarrow$P, $\uparrow$C = **Content or bored.** Despite having plenty of resources and strengths to use, your low amount of pressure might be intentionally created to not have to handle challenges, or it could be a source of distress.

$\uparrow$P, $\uparrow$C = **Engaged.** In this scenario, high resources and potential meet the high degree of pressure. This could be an optimal scenario for you and an opportunity to experience flow states where you are "in the zone."

$\downarrow$P, $\downarrow$C = **Autopilot.** Without much pressure or capacity use, there is little choice but to go through the motions in life, not particularly present to or challenged by much around you. This could be a source of distress.

Again, these are gross generalities for the many layers of pressure and capacity that are at play. They are offered to give you a general idea of where you might fall or the direction in which you might be heading.

This chapter will emphasize the hidden potential of our character strength capacities, particularly the fact that the enhancement and use of these capacities is a central element of stress management and can transcend our pressure levels, whether they be low, moderate, or high. Our strength capacities can release our best external resources and our internal abilities and passions.

Boosting Your Full Capacity

Do you believe you can turn your stress into something positive? The more you enhance your strength capacities, the more likely it is that you will answer yes to this question.

Chapter 2 raised a couple key points that are important reminders as you make your way through this chapter:

1.   All 24 character strengths matter.

2.   Your signature strengths matter most (in many situations).

When you think about stress management, you never want to lose sight of either of these points. You will be enhancing your capacity whether you *build upon* those strengths that are already natural and strong for you or whether you *build up* your nonsignature strengths. All 24 of your character strengths serve as energy reserves that you can tap into or develop. As I mentioned in the book's introduction, *your strengths are already there, waiting to be used by you.* But sometimes this might not feel true—you can feel weak, lost, and anything but empowered.

I recall a story about Amaya, a novice martial artist who was training with a master in a small group at a karate studio. She had been training for two years but felt insecure and unsure of herself. Her group consisted mostly of stronger boys, all of whom were further along in their training. The time came each week during the class when the students were to pair off and spar with each other, practicing their karate skills one-on-one by doing the punches, kicks, and blocks that they'd been learning while in the simulation of an actual fight. They wore forearm and elbow pads, applied tape and light padding over their hands and feet, and adhered to certain rules, like no hitting below the belt or above the neck.

Amaya dreaded this part of the class. She always felt like it was a sanctioned way for her to get beat up in a controlled setting. She persevered because she knew it would make her tougher and because it was just part of the class.

One week as she squared up with her male opponent, her master turned to her and said, "Hold up! Are you ready?"

"Yes, sir."

"You don't look ready," observed the master.

"I'm in my fighter's stance, sir. I'm ready," Amaya explained.

"Do you remember what's inside you?"

"Sir?"

"Do you remember what's inside you?" he repeated loudly.

"Uh, okay, yes," she muttered.

"Tell me."

"I am strong," she said in almost a whisper. But she was relieved that she'd at least had something to say.

"What?"

"I am stronger than I know," she said, not believing the words, but trying to get through this exchange as quickly as possible without all her fellow students hearing.

"Say what you feel. Look inside. Then speak."

Amaya paused. She wanted to do as her master asked. But she wasn't sure what to do or say. Would she say the wrong thing? At the very least, she figured, she could just repeat herself. She stood there, in position, sensing her master's firm yet encouraging presence, knowing the rest of the class was waiting on her. She felt her body in that moment—it felt solid and tough; the two years of training had done her well. She was aware of the surprisingly calm and concentrated state of her mind. She noticed warmth radiating within her. Something turned inside her. She felt a chill. Then, turning her head slightly in the direction of her master, she looked him in the eyes and spoke loudly:

"I'm stronger than I can even possibly know!" The words came out firm and powerful. She commanded them. Owned them. And actually believed them.

"Now you're ready," said the master.

We could argue that Amaya had turned to inner character strengths such as self-regulation, bravery, perseverance, and maybe even zest, hope, and love. The particular strengths matter less than the takeaways of finding empowerment at times of stress, discovering strength when you don't even know or believe it's there, and realizing that there is always a strength that can be accessed. We just need to remember to look.

Sometimes we need a reminder to not overlook or forget about our strength capacities. At other times we might need to practice using a strength—deliberately rehearsing a strength. In either case, character strengths are like muscles. When you exercise them, they get stronger and grow. When you don't exercise them, they stay the same or weaken.

Use a ROAD-MAP to Build Strength Capacity

Let's try out a tool called ROAD-MAP, which stands for seven straightforward behaviors that can be applied to *any* of the 24 character strengths to heighten stress capacity: reflect, observe, appreciate, discuss, monitor, ask, plan (Niemiec 2014). Each step offers an opportunity for strengths exploration and development.

Reflect: Consider your past strengths use. When have you used a particular strength at good times and at bad times? Name a situation in which you used quite a bit of bravery. What did bravery look like in action? When were you last curious with your spouse/partner? How did you express that curiosity? How was it received?

Observe: Sit back and take notice of others' behavior. How do people at the mall, on your work team, or on the theater stage express one or more character strengths? What do you notice about how they express the strength of gratitude or humility or teamwork?

Appreciate: Express value to someone for who they are; namely, for their strengths of character. Explain to someone why you value their strengths expression and how it is important to you. You might tell the friendly store clerk that their kindness warmed your heart and helped you let go of the pressures of your project deadline. You might tell your child that you appreciated their self-control at the restaurant.

Discuss: Have a deliberate conversation with someone about your strengths, their strengths, or a particular character strength. Explore one strength with the person. Take notice of the insights that flow as a result of the give-and-take dialogue.

Monitor: This refers to turning inward to watch your own behaviors. Track your strengths use. Make note of times and situations during the day when you use a strength, expectedly or unexpectedly. Or target one strength in particular and "count" your acts of creativity, of kindness, of humility.

Ask: Request help or support from others. Ask for feedback on your character strengths. When you know you'll be encountering a stressful situation at home, ask other people how they would use character strengths to handle the situation. Ask them how they would use the strength of perspective in the situation.

Plan: Make an action plan to use your strengths. Set a concrete goal for developing one of your strengths throughout this month. Plan to use one of your strengths during the busiest part of your day.

Which of the seven behaviors best aligns with your style of stress management? For example, some people love to talk about their stress, while others are more reflective and benefit from journaling or quiet contemplation. Which of the seven offers the best fit for you to practice your strengths? How so?

_____

_____

_____

Consider your signature strengths. Choose one signature strength and choose one of the seven behaviors. Brainstorm how you might link the two together in a beneficial way.

_____

_____

_____

_____

Consider your nonsignature strengths. Choose one nonsignature strength and choose one of the seven behaviors. Brainstorm how you might link the two together in a beneficial way.

_____

_____

_____

_____

When you consider all seven behaviors and all 24 character strengths, there's a multitude of possibilities for growing your strength capacities. This means that at virtually any moment of your life, you could discover a way to exercise your strengths. Keep the ROAD-MAP acronym handy so you can play with it each day!

Tap Abilities, Interests, and Resources for Capacity Building

You might recall from chapter 2 that there are many positive qualities you have in addition to your character strengths. Here we will focus on three types of them in relation to using your character strengths to manage stress, as understanding them will help you enhance your capacity.

Your Talents/Abilities

These are things you naturally do well. Are you a natural with the piano, a paintbrush, or a golf club? Do you have a knack for numbers, for comprehending what you read, or for relating to people?

Perhaps the best way to think about talents and abilities is to consider the work on multiple intelligences by Harvard psychologist Howard Gardner. Using a theory that has kept strong for well over three decades, he challenged the conventional thinking at the time that held that humans had just one general intelligence. Gardner (1983) argued that humans have many basic intelligences, and he categorized seven abilities in particular:

1. *Spatial:* The capacity for visual imagery, able to understand and transform spatial imagery. Displayed strongly in architects, city planners, sculptors, and billiard players.

2. *Logical-mathematical:* Competent with numbers and data, organizing ideas in abstract ways. Displayed strongly in math professors, accountants, quantitative researchers, and physicists.

3. *Bodily:* Kinesthetic capacity for one's body and its movement in space, having mastery and precise control over one's body. Shown in college/professional basketball players, skiers, dancers, surgeons, and yoga instructors.

4. *Linguistic:* Understanding, sensitivity to, and use of language—its function and meanings, able to be clear and precise with words and to offer different ways of explaining topics. Shown in poets, popular fiction writers, dialogue editors for movies, orators, and exemplary professors and teachers.

5. *Musical:* An ability to organize and produce sounds according to prescribed pitch and rhythm. Displayed strongly in singers, theatrical/musical performers, orchestra members, and other musicians.

6. *Personal:* Intrapersonal capacity to introspect and understand one's own thoughts, feelings, needs, desires, and hopes. Shown by clinical psychologists, novelists, filmmakers, and those who regularly meditate/contemplate.

7. *Social:* Interpersonal capacity to connect with people, to understand what makes people tick, to be tuned in to people's feelings and desires. Often displayed in social workers, pastors, salespersons, marketers, and politicians.

Each of these entails a problem-solving skill set that you might already be naturally using to manage stress or other difficulties in your life. These abilities can function independently from one another, so you can be high in one or two and low in others.

As you look at this list of seven intelligences, don't get caught up in extremist thinking— that is, concluding that you cannot relate to any because you're not in one of the professions listed or you're not an Olympic athlete or a hard scientist. Instead, look to see which one or two (or more) you relate to most.

Consider your accomplishments. If you examine what you have accomplished in your life and how you got to this point in your life, that can point to one or more of your abilities. Did you gain that award at work not only because you worked hard, but because you are very good at connecting with many people or are politically savvy? If so, that might say something about your social ability. Did you receive a substantial amount of praise when you performed in your tenth-grade musical? If so, then perhaps musical intelligence is a core ability for you.

Consider your intrigue. Which category is most intriguing to you? Those who have a particular ability are usually quite attuned to the display of that ability by others. If you are fascinated by biographies about scientists, then logical-mathematical ability may align nicely with you. If you marvel at wordsmiths who offer brilliant TED Talks, then you might have a good deal of linguistic ability. Think about who you admire, the people who are most memorable to you. We're often intrigued by abilities we possess ourselves.

WHAT ARE YOU GOOD AT?

Which of the seven abilities do you relate to most? Write down what you perceive to be your top ability:

_____

How do you express this ability in your daily life?

_____

_____

_____

_____

_____

Which of your character strengths helps you best express this ability? For example, self-regulation and perseverance help an athlete with a bodily ability to train day after day for the big event. The social worker taps into his strengths of fairness and kindness to connect with his clients as he uses his social ability. The architect, in using her spatial ability, expresses strong perspective to see the big picture of the building she is designing, along with substantial judgment/critical thinking to attend to the fine details and decisions that go into her drawings.

_____

_____

_____

_____

_____

How does this combination of your chosen ability with accompanying character strengths help you manage stress? Explore one stressor in your life in which your ability and your character strengths played a central role in helping you resolve or manage it:

_____

_____

_____

_____

_____

Your Interests

Interests are topics or activities that you pursue with passion. Sometimes you partake in them for distraction, sometimes for pure enjoyment, and sometimes for meaning; but regardless of the reason, your interests are sure to engage you! They hold your attention and enliven you. They can emerge in any context—work, school, social, home, community—and can be private or public. Popular interests include reading, watching television, fishing, gardening, following social media, and spending time with family. But each of these examples can get far more specific, like reading magazines on mechanics, watching TV series about zombies, ice fishing in Canada, growing herbs and spices for daily meals, editing photos for Instagram, and having a family movie night every Friday.

At work, I'm passionate about teaching others about such topics as mindfulness, spirituality, and character strengths. At home, I'm interested in engaging in creative play with my kids. And when I'm alone, my interests involve collectibles, playing online chess, and watching positive psychology movies. When my interests and passions are ignited, so are my character strengths. My curiosity is piqued to learn something new, my hope elevates to attain something new for a collection, and my creativity, love, and humor are unleashed as I play with my children. Upon closer examination, in fact, it is often my character strengths that are fueling my interests. For example, as I teach, my strength of zest drives my enthusiasm for the topic at hand and my hope strength leads me to see the potential positive impact I'm making. In turn, I am inspired to take on additional teaching gigs.

As you consider your own interests below, it's helpful to ask: What do you do in your leisure time? How you spend your time (productively or unproductively, doing routine tasks, being lazy) can tell you something not only about your interests, but also about your stress level. For instance, if your go-to stress relief activity is to veg out in front of the TV, then watching television is probably an important interest area for you. To further help you zero in on your primary interests, answer these questions: If you had time to designate each week for leisure, what would you do? If you could do any fun activity right now, what would you select?

WHAT ARE YOU PASSIONATE ABOUT?

Consider your interest areas in one or more domains of your life. What do you most want to spend your leisure time doing? What is most fun for you? List your top three interests:

_____

_____

_____

Which character strengths are you using most when you express these three passions? How do your character strengths help you ignite these interests?

_____

_____

_____

How often do you tap into these three interest areas? Does it seem like it might be important for you to arrange your life to have more time for one or more of them? If yes, how might you take action in that direction?

_____

_____

_____

How does this combination of your interests and accompanying character strengths help you at times of stress? Explore one stressor in your life in which your interests and character strengths played a central role in helping you resolve or manage it:

_____

_____

_____

Your Resources

People, institutions, communities, and other networks of support that exist outside of you comprise your external resources. These, too, serve to boost your strength capacity and play an important role in believing you can handle and manage stress.

If you have a lot of resources, then you perhaps have several close friends, take part in classes to enhance your learning, have family members you can turn to and rely on, and live in a trusting neighborhood. Being part of institutions that support you also contributes to this capacity, such as volunteer groups, religious or spiritual groups, and groups affiliated with your local schools or businesses. Those who suffer from an addiction will swear by the importance of regular attendance at a support group. Not only does this resource aid recovery, but it builds internal capacities like empathy, wisdom, courage, and resilience.

Character strengths help you to connect within any particular resource. Your strengths of social intelligence and teamwork, for example, can assist you in navigating a new volunteer group, while your strengths of forgiveness and love can be practiced in the presence of others at a spiritual gathering. The resource itself may be a direct outlet for character strength expression, such as kindness if you volunteer for the Red Cross or judgment/critical thinking and bravery if you are involved with the Girl Scouts or Boy Scouts.

Our resources serve as deep wells of support that sustain us through challenging times. Here's what seventy-two-year old Edna had to say about the stress of losing her husband of forty-five years and the value of returning to her strengths in that time of need:

> After I lost Frank, I didn't know what to do. I just sat at home. It was difficult to eat or to sleep. I wanted to be alone. My friends would come by to visit, but I didn't want to see them. Everything was a struggle. Then I remembered my volunteer work at the downtown shelter and soup kitchen. I decided to go back to helping out two times a week. On the first day of my return, all the other volunteers and organizers sure were glad to see me! It was meaningful for me to be back as part of the volunteer team. But what I was most surprised by were the people receiving the services, most of whom were homeless. They were overjoyed. Most of them came and gave me a big hug. I was tearful by all this. And, of course, the outpouring of support I received from them about the loss of my dear Frank was wonderful. I can't really describe it. I felt the love and warmth. After a week or two of volunteering, I was ready to return to the rest of my support network, such as my friends and my children and grandchildren. I don't know what I'd do without everybody.

WHAT ARE YOUR EXTERNAL SUPPORTS?

Who are your supports? Consider your work, home, social, and community life. List the names of the people you feel supported by and who are part of your support network:

_____

_____

_____

What are your institutional or group supports? Name any business, nonprofit or volunteer organization, or educational or spiritual group that is a support to you:

_____

_____

_____

Considering the supports you listed in the previous two questions, what are the character strengths you use to connect with these people and institutions? Which character strengths help you thrive in these relationships?

_____

_____

_____

How does this combination of your resources and accompanying character strengths help you at times of stress? Explore one stressor in your life in which your resources and character strengths played a central role in helping you resolve or manage it:

_____

_____

_____

Putting All the Strengths Together

This passage aptly captures the interrelationship of character strengths combined with other types of human strengths as a valuable way to augment capacity and handle stress:

There's a moving story of a young man named Benny, a talented and influential presenter to businesses and youth education programs. Benny was married, had two children, a strong spiritual community, and many friends. He was a charismatic man with many talents, resources, and interests. Unfortunately, job stress, financial struggles, and peer temptation began to impact Benny, and he turned to selling drugs to supplement his income. Benny noticed his resources began to dwindle as he prioritized the wrong crowd and avoided his childhood friends. His situation worsened as he sunk deep into this dangerous lifestyle. One day, when walking to his car in broad daylight, he was shot several times in the stomach and arms. Benny underwent seventeen surgeries and meanwhile lost all his financial savings, could no longer hold down his job, his wife left him, and he became estranged from his children and church community. These circumstances were accompanied by deep feelings of depression which almost always means *anhedonia*—a loss of interest in what he was previously interested in. As the young man recounted his story to me, he also shared a stirring insight that came to him one day while lying in a hospital bed staring at the ceiling: "I had lost everything, the people in my life, my money, my job, and even use of parts of my body, but one thing I did not lose was my core strengths. These could not be taken away from me." He was speaking about his bravery, honesty, creativity, social intelligence, and hopefulness.

In summary, talents can be squandered, resources can be quickly lost, interests wane and change, skills diminish over time, but when all seems completely lost, we still have our character strengths. When focused on, our character strengths crystallize and evolve and can integrate with these other positive qualities to contribute to the greater good (Niemiec 2018, 17).

Now that you've learned a wide range of strategies for boosting capacities, let's turn to the other side of the stress equation: the pressure side.

Handling Pressures: Reframing or Reducing?

Ice cream? Yum! Ice cream only and all the time? Ugh! It is not that stress is bad for us, it is how we manage stress that matters. In using the stress equation, ice cream can be viewed as a "physical" pressure. The sugar and calorie intake can impact the body and bring on some duress. This varies by each person—someone with diabetes will experience the "stress pressure" of ice cream (even one serving) far more than a healthy eighteen-year-old.

What we know about stress pressure is that the "right" amount is constructive, helping us grow, and can even lead to a special and very positive subjective experience called "flow"—when we are completely absorbed in what we are doing, losing track of time and emerging with a sense of productivity and satisfaction. Too much pressure can be destructive, causing a breakdown or degradation in our physical and/or psychological health. Too little pressure can also be maladaptive, as seen in the person who is bored with life and finding little challenge or fulfillment in anything.

As this chapter unfolds, we're learning that we can tap into and grow our various capacities and experience not only personal growth but also greater competence and confidence in handling stress and seeing the positive in it. This section will address the "pressure" side of the equation, and there are multiple ways of doing so: we can face and accept the good of the pressure and learn to excel because of it; we can work to lower the pressure; and we can increase our pressure when it is too low. Let's explore each of these in turn.

Excelling Under Pressure: Allowing and Accepting Stress

There is a principle in clinical psychology that espouses to "go with the resistance." This means that if a client is insisting on viewing a problem a certain way or is vehemently disagreeing with a therapist about quitting smoking or eating snacks at night, then it might behoove the therapist to agree rather than to stay in the back-and-forth cycle of conflict or disagreement. A therapist might say, "Okay, it's your choice, I won't fight you on the smoking cessation anymore." The therapist might even incorporate a character strength to reframe and observe, "Wow, you are really persevering with this argument. You seem to overcome every obstacle I throw at you! And your zest and energy for your perspective are also quite high. These character strengths, perseverance and zest, are tremendously important strengths to have. Do you find that you use these regularly in your life in other ways?"

Often, this results in a diffusion of tension for the client and some experience of an opening toward a new way of looking at themselves. Just as the person trained in the martial arts of judo or aikido knows to make use of the opponent's energy rather than trying to overpower them or fight force with force, you can see and use the energy of stress. Instead of fighting against stress, see the good in it. Notice how it motivates you toward action. You would never accomplish anything in life without it. You wouldn't push yourself to connect in relationships without it. You probably wouldn't find much meaning and purpose in life without it.

To deny that stress is present is to lose touch with reality, so an important first step in excelling under pressure is to acknowledge and name the presence of a stressor or a tension in your body or the challenge of a new work project. This is a way of subtly saying, "I see you, stress," rather than avoiding it, denying it, or minimizing it.

From this acknowledgment of stress, we move into acceptance. Just like the therapist accepting the client's views, we can accept that stress is here in the moment. The seventh-grade student accepts that doing two hours of homework a night is a stressor that is simply part of the reality of going to school and important for learning, while the couple bickering at home about who is going to do the dishes this week can accept that everyday tensions like this are part of the reality of having a marriage and of the growth in any relationship.

After acceptance comes action. So what will you do now with this stress? How will you take action in a positive way? The perspective here is "action with strengths," finding a way to bring in one or more of your character strengths to see the stress in a different way. Recent research studies show we can use our strengths to manage our stress and improve our coping in life in general, including handling stress in specific situations, like at work (Harzer and Ruch 2015).

TAKE ON STRESS THE "TRIPLE-A WAY"

Consider one stressor in your life. Look at it anew using the "Triple-A Way," in which you *acknowledge* the stress, *accept* the stress, and take *action* with the stress. How will you practice fully acknowledging stress—what will you say to yourself? How will you accept stress—what might be your self-talk in the moment when you are accepting the reality of stress without trying to get rid of it? What action will you take with your strengths to better manage this stressor?

Name one stressor: _____

_____

1. Acknowledge stress: _____

_____

2. Accept stress: _____

_____

3. Action with strengths: _____

_____

The Problem of High Pressure: Lowering Stress When Life Is Too Much

In the process of perceiving your capacities and resources, you may, at times, overestimate them. This results in taking on too many demands, possibly to the point of "breaking" and feeling that you are overwhelmed, that you are at or beyond your capacity. You may also begin to feel inadequate, incompetent, lazy, or not talented enough. In reality, you have simply "bitten off more than you can chew" at the moment.

Additionally, you can underestimate demands, thinking that a work project or homework assignment will be easy to complete and won't take up much time. Unwittingly taking on a large amount of new pressure can quickly make you feel like you are "in over your head" and unable to be effective.

Consider Marjorie, a full-time office manager and single mother of two boys, who was quick to say yes to any new project that came her way. She went "above and beyond" at work, took classes in the evenings, and regularly volunteered to be the driver for her kids and their friends to their various extracurricular activities throughout the week. She thrived under pressure and her hectic schedule, viewing stress as a necessary and beneficial part of her growth. Some weeks, however, it felt like too much for Marjorie. She'd get headaches, she'd eat poorly, and she wouldn't get enough sleep. She could tell when an intense amount of pressure was really getting to her because she'd become easily irritated by her kids, with whom she was otherwise very compassionate and gentle.

Using the Triple-A Way framework, Marjorie readily acknowledged her stress, well aware of when the intensity level increased. Marjorie also accepted her various stressors as not only part of her reality, but as a welcomed reality in her life. The third step, however—taking action with strengths—was not something to which Marjorie was particularly attuned.

In examining the 24 character strengths, it became clear to her that she could develop more prudence to plan for better health habits during difficult weeks. She was already adept at expressing her prudence at work and with her kids' schedules, but she hadn't previously considered using this strength to plan meals, protect sleep time, and get proper exercise. Her strength of perspective assisted her in looking at the larger picture of her life and making decisions about taking on even more responsibilities at certain times. To deploy perspective whenever she encountered a potential new activity or commitment, she first asked herself: "In the big picture of the life of my family, will this new thing be more helpful or harmful for me and my sons?" Asking this question helped Marjorie take the reins of stress and either directly increase or decrease her pressure levels. It became *her* decision.

NEW POTENTIAL PRESSURES: WILL THEY HELP OR HARM?

Think of a life challenge that you are considering embarking on or a request someone has made of you. Make sure it's something to which you can freely say yes or no—not, for example, an assignment your boss has given you. Instead, write down below something like a neighbor asking you to do a daily favor, a teacher proposing "extra credit" work, or a new volunteer opportunity that has just opened up in your community.

_____

_____

_____

_____

As you think about this challenge or project/request, consider the demands that will likely be placed upon you. How much pressure would this amount to? What is the time commitment? How might this impact your health, your relationships, your leisure time, your family, your work?

_____

_____

_____

_____

Is taking on this new challenge/project/request something that will veer more in the direction of helping you or harming you? Explain your answer:

_____

_____

_____

_____

Whether you chose "helping" or "harming" in the previous question, consider your character strengths. How might your character strength capacities support you if you accept the new pressure or reject it?

_____

_____

_____

_____

The Problem of Low Pressure: Give Yourself More Stress!

Interestingly, too few demands or too little pressure can lead to distress. This is evidenced in the research on sedentary behavior, which shows that a lifestyle of sitting with minimal movement and activity increases the risk of various cancers and is more dangerous to the body than smoking (Schmid and Colditz 2014). Just as too much exercise might lead to injury, too little movement can also have a negative effect. Each person must find their balance.

Boredom and apathy can take a toll on your body and mind. They can set you up for a pattern of not challenging yourself and avoiding situations that might contain any modicum of stress, rigor, or sustained effort. A bored or apathetic person does indeed have strength capacities they can access and activate to become engaged.

If you feel you are lost in a low-pressure lifestyle, you might be languishing—simply going through the motions of life and not feeling very good mentally and not connecting much socially. This is what happened to Hank, a thirty-eight-year-old man with a girlfriend and no kids, who was laid off from his job as a construction worker. He lived in a small town where work was scarce. Rather than looking for a different line of work that might suit his abilities and strengths, he turned to his couch. He felt confused, disengaged, and discouraged. This was reinforced by two of his former coworkers, who'd also been laid off and took a similar approach.

Week after week went by, and Hank just sat around, went to bars, spent time with his girlfriend when she was off work, and hung out with friends. Occasionally, he looked at job postings online, but not with any serious effort. Hank thought he was living an easy, pressure-free life, with no demands and almost no responsibilities. But after a few months of this, he realized he was miserable. His inactivity had led to him not taking care of his body. It was not until he began to attend to his "mind" strengths, such as his curiosity and his desire to learn, that he was able to jump-start himself back on track. He used his character strengths to learn a new trade and attain an online certification. Furthermore, his curiosity also led him to pursue new interests, hobbies, and exercise routines.

LOW-PRESSURE REMEDY: USE YOUR THINKING-ORIENTED STRENGTHS

You'll recall that the virtue of wisdom in the VIA Classification is stocked with *cognitive*, or thinking-oriented, strengths. These strengths of the mind include creativity, curiosity, judgment/critical thinking, love of learning, and perspective. Targeting these strengths can be useful in challenging yourself to experience more pressure in life and pursue areas of interest.

Explore the questions below, each targeting a different character strength.

Creativity. A key part of this strength is that it involves *divergent thinking*—coming up with many different ways to solve a problem. Take a moment to view the phenomenon of "low pressure" as a problem. Now list at least three ways you could solve this problem:

_____

_____

_____

_____

Curiosity. Name something that is going well in your life (health, relationship, hobby, sport, art/music expression, family, work). Take a moment to be curious about this area. Be interested and intrigued by it. How did this area emerge for you? What has been your role in contributing to the positives in this area? How might the successes be expanded upon in your life? Explore your thoughts here:

_____

_____

_____

_____

Judgment/Critical Thinking. Take a close look at a time, now or in the past, when you felt very low pressure. Examine the details of your life in low-pressure mode. What are/were the specific positive and negative elements of this time?

_____

_____

_____

_____

Love of Learning. What topics or subject areas have always captured your interest? Don't hesitate to write down anything that comes to mind. Be sure to consider areas that interested you five or ten years (or longer) ago. How might you reinvigorate one of these areas?

_____

_____

_____

_____

Perspective. Consider a time when you experienced stress and it benefited you. What did you gain from the stressor? What did you learn?

_____

_____

_____

_____

Taken together, these five strengths pack a lot of wisdom. This wisdom can most certainly be applied to low-pressure stress.

Making Plans to Combat Stress

If there's one thing we know, it's that we'll all experience pressures and demands to some degree in life. Why not plan for your stressors? Map out how you will make the most of your strength capacities? Your character strengths are the central part of your overall capacity to tilt the stress equation in the right direction. They are the fuel that ignites your passions, talents, and resources. They are therefore essential to the management of pressure and capacity.

For this activity, think of three stressors that you are experiencing right now or that you will likely experience in the next week—for example, coping with a tension headache, traveling to a city you'd rather not visit, or having a difficult meeting with your child's teacher. Then, following the example given as a cue, map out how your various strength capacities can be tapped into or enhanced to manage the stress.

Stressor	Character Strengths	How I Could Use My Strengths	Other Qualities: My Abilities, Interests, or Resources	How I Could Use My Other Qualities			
My child has not been studying for a test that will be given this week.	Creativity Social intelligence Self-regulation	I'll come up with new ways to encourage him to study, including rewards and working alongside him. Rather than argue with him about it, I'll ask him his study plans, his perspective, and thoughts about the subject matter. I'll tell him about how I've applied discipline in a different area, that of exercising regularly.	Social (ability) His best friend (resource)	I'll use my social talent to casually connect with him and understand his feelings while we're eating dinner together. I'll ask him how his best friend, who is a good student, approaches homework in this class. I may explore the idea of them studying together to serve as a catalyst.			

Learn. Practice. SHARE.

In this chapter, you've learned a variety of ways to boost your many capacities, including your character strengths, talents/abilities, interests, and resources, as well as to manage the pressures you are under. Your practice has involved examining stressors in new ways that align with your various capacities.

Before moving on to chapter 4, consider this: What is most important for you to share with others right now?

Share an insight, practice, or goal with one person. You might share the stress equation with a friend or discuss with your spouse how the two of you can increase your capacity together as a team. Explore your "share" below and note with whom you will connect:

_____

_____

_____

_____

_____

CHAPTER 4

Learn to Spot Strengths

We are quick to hyperfocus on troubles and to take our positives for granted. The positive events of our life can float past us like a burst of wind we never knew was there. We believe we are noticing the positives along with the negatives, but that's not likely the case. See what I mean for yourself by filling out the grid below. List three positive experiences you had in the last twenty-four hours, along with a few details about each.

	Positive experience/ situation in the last day	What was the positive you noticed?	What character strengths were involved?	What did you learn? Was it helpful with managing stress?
Example	While walking my dog, I stopped to talk with my neighbor.	I noticed how friendly he was. We had a fun conversation.	Zest/energy (in me); humor and kindness (in him).	I felt better when I took the time to connect with someone new. I'd like to make more efforts like this. My shoulder tension eased afterward.

	Positive experience/ situation in the last day	What was the positive you noticed?	What character strengths were involved?	What did you learn? Was it helpful with managing stress?
1				
2				
3				

Was it easy or difficult for you to do this activity? Did it take a while to come up with the examples? Most people find it surprisingly challenging. But if I were to ask you to recall three stressors from the past day, you could probably list at least ten in no time at all, right?

It's easier to notice the stressors in life. We can all do better at looking for the good, the positive, the virtuous, the ethical, and the strengths in ourselves and in the people around us. A focal point of this chapter will be targeting the development of this skill—a skill referred to as *strengths-spotting*.

"Know Thyself" by Knowing Thy Strengths

Joey, a medical equipment salesman, faced a difficult problem. His boss told him he had to give a speech in front of a hundred people on behalf of their team, and Joey hated public speaking. He avoided it at all costs. His boss knew this about Joey. Was he testing him? Perhaps he had no one else to turn to? Regardless, Joey had no choice. He loved his job and wanted to keep it. The speech would be to existing and potential future customers. It was important. Joey's anxiety was through the roof. Would he make mistakes and mess up the business? Would he even be able to speak once he got out there? How could he face a hundred sets of eyes staring at him?

Joey reminded himself about his signature strengths. He asked himself, *How might my top strength of perspective help me see the bigger picture?*

First off, he thought, *I don't have to see this as a "problem"; instead, I can view it as a challenge—something difficult, but something I can do. It's actually an opportunity!* Joey reframed the speech as an opportunity to educate potential customers about what he knew, to show his skills and knowledge to his boss, and to be helpful to his team.

Then he considered his signature strength of gratitude. Joey always felt enlivened when he expressed this strength. *Why not share my gratitude to all the existing customers in the room?* he thought. *Early on in the talk, when I'll likely be most nervous, I'll thank our customers and take time to express why our team is so grateful for their loyalty.* He realized this would bring the added benefits of connecting with the audience right from the start and portraying the company as a warm and appreciative business partner.

Finally, Joey reminded himself of his third signature strength: humor. *I do like to make people laugh, and telling stories and jokes comes easy to me,* he reflected. *My talk is somewhat serious so I can't go overboard with humor, but I can work in a couple jokes and a funny story that happened to me while on the job.* So Joey planned to start off with some lightheartedness by making a funny comment about the environment they'd be in. If he laughed at his own jokes, it would bring some stress relief to his body. And if the audience didn't laugh, he decided he wouldn't be bothered by this—he'd just continue to mix the informative with the humorous.

In this way, Joey found that he could bring himself—who he was and what came most naturally to him—right into the experience. His spotting of strengths in himself helped him transform what initially seemed like an awful situation into a chance to use his signature strengths to face it and perhaps even enjoy parts of it.

Spotting strengths takes practice, but it is a skill anyone can develop. It occurs on two levels: spotting strengths in yourself and spotting strengths in others.

Ready for a challenge? Let's start with the harder level—spotting strengths in yourself. When I ask audiences across the globe which level they find easier to do, 90 percent of hands go up claiming it's easier to spot strengths in others. Looking within can feel subjective and uncertain, whereas seeing kindness or fairness in someone else, right in front of our eyes, has a clarity and objectivity about it. It seems more real. But learning to apply the language of strengths to yourself will serve you well when you interact with others and will boost your confidence during encounters with others who are also displaying their strengths. It's a good growth step in the wise adage to "know thyself."

To begin strengths-spotting, you'll want to have a sense of the positives you're looking for. This is where being familiar with the foundational language of strengths is crucial. You've been building your knowledge of the 24 strengths since you began reading this workbook, and it's been growing chapter by chapter. It might be helpful to have at hand a copy of the VIA Classification in the introduction, which contains all of the strengths and their corresponding definitions. For once you know what you're looking for, you can set the intention to spot strengths in action—in other words, you can put on "strengths goggles" to help you see past the boring routines of life to discover your strengths and to find exceptions and positives within your stress and discomfort. Wearing "strengths goggles" is not Pollyannaish or one-sided; rather, it brings in a perspective of reality that is often missed in today's world.

Strengths-Spotting in This Moment

You can start practicing spotting strengths in yourself this very moment. What character strengths are you using right now as you read this chapter? Maybe you are using prudence, because you plan to read only for another fifteen minutes. Maybe you are using perseverance, because you are tired but you'll still keep going. Maybe you are using creativity to review the list of strengths and think about yours in a new way. As in most situations, any of the 24 character strengths are possible. Which are you using right now and how?

Strength #1: _____

_____

Strength #2: _____

_____

Strength #3: _____

_____

To spot character strengths is to add substance to any situation. Consider the two stories below, in which the exact same thing happens in each:

Version 1: I woke up this morning, had breakfast, and got dressed. As I drove to work, I encountered a lot of bad traffic and the drivers on the road seemed angry and aggressive, often cutting me off. I arrived late for a work meeting and therefore apologized to my boss.

Version 2: I woke up this morning with a feeling of zest, excited to start the day. For breakfast, I used prudence to be thoughtful and careful about my choices considering my high cholesterol, so I had an egg-white omelet with fresh vegetables with my coffee. As I got dressed, I paused to marvel at the smoothness of the material and vibrancy of the colors of my clothes (appreciating the beauty and excellence), which my spouse had pressed for me the preceding day. I felt spurts of gratitude for my spouse. As I drove to work, I encountered a lot of bad traffic and the drivers on the road seemed angry and aggressive, often cutting me off. I practiced forgiveness, letting go of these minor irritants as they occurred, while being aided by perspective, seeing the possible bigger picture that perhaps some had emergencies to attend to and others were experiencing anger and therefore in need of kindness and compassion. I arrived late for a work meeting, and feeling a bit embarrassed, I mustered up the bravery to apologize to my boss. I was honest about the situation and was clear to self-regulate my urge to blame the traffic for my lateness and instead took responsibility for not having planned ahead enough to account for the delay.

The plot of each version is identical, but a significant difference emerges in the details, the nuances. The first recounting is mundane, whereas the second is more interesting and engaging. The second version offers insight into the narrator—how this person approaches life in general and in specific situations. It's the ten character strengths mentioned directly that infuse the story with greater meaning. They lead to a deeper understanding of the person's psyche and their relationships, allowing the listener/reader to generate more questions.

One of the best ways to learn about your strongest qualities is to deploy a strategy that psychologists refer to as *self-monitoring*—closely observing your thoughts, feelings, and behaviors over a specified period of time. Self-monitoring is a science-based method used to help people improve in a range of areas, such as anger management, emotion management, and stress management. You can apply this tool to learn more about your character strengths and the subtle ways in which they appear in your life.

Self-Monitor Your Strengths

Begin to track the many ways in which your character strengths appear in your daily life by using the self-monitoring sheet below (also available for repeated use at http://www.newhar binger.com/42808). First, decide on a period of time in which you will track your strengths. This might be one morning, one day, or one week. Next, decide how you will remind yourself to keep up with tracking your strengths. A smartphone alarm or timer set to chime at various intervals throughout your chosen period of time usually works well. Whenever you hear the chime, pause to check in on the strengths you are using, no matter how subtly, and how you are using them in the situation at hand.

Day/Time	Current Activity	Character Strength(s)	How I'm Using My Strengths	Other Comments (emotions felt, obstacles to using strengths, and so forth)
Tuesday/2:30 p.m.	Team meeting	Curiosity; leadership	Asking various questions of teammates; offered to lead a new project	Felt excited; one obstacle was I didn't want to step on teammates' toes in offering to lead the project

By self-monitoring in this way, you're starting a good habit of not only acknowledging the existence of character strengths, but actually seeing these qualities of goodness in your own behaviors. Keep up with building the skill of strengths-spotting in yourself, and it will become second nature to you. It will also be a cinch for you to spot strengths in others, which we'll turn to now.

Become a Skilled Strengths-Spotter

Lisa could see that Emily was struggling. Emily's learning disability was getting the best of her. She was mentally fatigued and frustrated, not sure how to figure out the math problems being presented to her. As Emily's tutor, Lisa could sense the frustration. It was palpable, particularly in Emily's crunched-up facial expressions, not to mention her occasional foot stomping. Lisa decided to take a different tactic.

"Let's just pause for a moment. Stop and take a breath," she advised.

Emily was caught off guard, which tempered her frustration for the moment.

"I want to point something out to you," Lisa said. "I see so much bravery in you, Emily. You have to deal with so many challenges, but you face them all."

Emily quieted to listen, stunned by the observation.

Lisa continued, "Day after day, you go to class, knowing that you'll be facing struggles with learning new material and that you're in a class with a teacher who doesn't seem to understand you or offer any help. And the material gets harder and harder with every class. You know you'll get odd looks and occasional jokes from classmates and feel the stress build. Yet you keep going, day after day, trying your best. I'm amazed by your bravery—your courage to step in and take it. You don't even hesitate! I admire how you confront all your adversities and keep going. You inspire me to be brave in my own life, like with confronting my parents about some things."

Emily became tearful. No one had ever pointed out a strength in her so directly, and certainly not a strength like bravery. She could see the truth in what Lisa was saying. It was both accurate and powerful.

To hear about ourselves through the words of others is to see ourselves in a new light. A few words of strengths-spotting in Emily were enough to point her in a different direction. Lisa continued to point out additional strengths she observed in Emily as they worked together, such as Emily's perseverance in sticking with a difficult math problem and her honesty in being forthright about her difficulties. In turn, Emily began to spot strengths in Lisa! She pointed out Lisa's creativity in never failing to come up with a new way of solving a math problem or helping Emily learn. Their relationship—and their work together—reached a new level.

When spotting strengths in others, we can learn from Lisa by following the three steps she took with Emily:

1. *Label the strength.* Name the character strength being observed. Lisa pointed out the strength of bravery, then later spotted perseverance and honesty.

2. *Give your rationale.* Offer an explanation for the strength you are spotting. Note the behavioral "evidence" for your label. Lisa offered a number of examples of Emily's bravery, such as facing the challenges of a difficult classroom with an unhelpful teacher and unkind peers.

3. *Offer appreciation.* Express your value for the person and their strengths. Validate their strengths use. Explain how it has a positive effect on you. Lisa described how she finds Emily's bravery inspiring and that it might serve as a catalyst for using her own bravery with her parents.

The interesting point about spotting strengths in others is that you can practice it anywhere, anytime. You might be reading a novel, watching television, posting on Facebook or Instagram, sitting in a classroom listening to a lecture, or e-mailing a friend at work. You can hone your skill and look for the positive, searching for the character strengths in the person or in the story's character.

When you are looking for potential strengths, there are some clues—both verbal and nonverbal—that can help you detect that a strength might be present. When one or more of these are displayed, it can serve as a green light for you to pay close attention and listen for potential strengths.

Nonverbal clues for strengths	*Verbal clues for strengths*
Improved posture	Speech becomes more rapid/excited
Eyes light up	Speech becomes less rapid/excited
Increased eye contact	Speech becomes more/less slowed/ methodical/reflective
General lift in bodily energy	
More frequent hand gestures	Increased use of positive words
Body leaning forward	Improved clarity of speech
More open stance (uncrossing arms/legs)	Stronger/firmer voice
Smiling/laughing	Wider vocabulary
Expression of positive emotions (such as joy)	More confidence in speaking
	Speaking to various details of a story/situation

Seeing Strengths in Others

Spotting strengths in others can be particularly engaging and energizing—for you and the other person! Research studies show that we experience increased well-being when we have strength-based conversations, such as sharing positive news that happens in our day (Gable et al. 2004; Reis et al. 2010). So you will likely benefit from extending your habit of perceiving strengths to other people.

Practice observing any person—a family member, neighbor, or coworker. You can start to fine-tune your observation skills with people you don't know first, like figures in the news or characters on a TV show or in a movie or book. A colleague and I honed our own strengths-spotting skills by cataloging and discussing over 1,500 movies to observe, understand, and witness character strengths in action (Niemiec and Wedding 2014).

For any person in your life or in the media, what character strengths are they displaying most strongly? How can you tell they are using a character strength—what verbal or nonverbal clues do they express? Explore a few examples below, from a variety of life situations. Don't forget to offer a rationale or explanation for each strength you spot.

Family Member: _____

_____

_____

Neighbor: _____

_____

_____

Colleague: _____

_____

_____

Famous Person: _____

_____

_____

Fictional Character: _____

_____

_____

Spot Strengths Everywhere

You've been practicing spotting strengths in yourself and others that you've observed in the past. But let's make this practice part of your future daily routine by downloading and regularly completing this worksheet at http://www.newharbinger.com/42808.

Type of Strengths-Spotting: Self or Others	Activity	Character Strengths Spotted	Rationale/Evidence for Strengths Spotted	Emotions Felt/ New Learning
Self	E-mailing a friend	Hope; social intelligence	My friend was struggling with a problem. My message was empathic to her feelings (social intelligence) and optimistic (hopeful) because I pointed out several of her positive qualities.	I felt joy as I offered support and felt gratitude that she'd shared her problem with me. I learned that I use social intelligence much more often than I realize!

Type of Strengths-Spotting: Self or Others	Activity	Character Strengths Spotted	Rationale/Evidence for Strengths Spotted	Emotions Felt/ New Learning

Your strengths-spotting practice is starting to move at full tilt! Now, in order to become even more well rounded with your strengths fluency, personal understanding, and applications, let's reverse the process by turning to others' views of your strengths.

Build in the Views of Others

Another means of employing strengths-spotting is to place yourself on the receiving end of the lens of others. What character strengths are others spotting in you? Learning from others is a crucial way to further explore your character strengths. There are always insights that emerge from this kind of learning, because sometimes others know more about us than we do ourselves! Think back to the conversation between Lisa and Emily, for instance, in which Emily didn't seem to know she was brave. It would never have occurred to her to think of herself or to describe herself that way. But all it took to wake Emily up to this quality in herself was for Lisa to spot it and cite an example or two. Emily walked away with a "revised" vision of herself.

The best way to attain this kind of input from others, in a formal way, is to use what's called a "360° form." This is a standard way of providing feedback in top organizations around the world. Rather than gathering feedback from only one source, it involves each employee receiving feedback from multiple sources in their work environment, not only their boss/supervisor, but also subordinates, colleagues, and customers. Each of these sources provides feedback to the employee on how they perceive their work performance, which yields a comprehensive portrait.

Why not take this approach with character strengths? I asked myself. So I developed a Character Strengths 360° tool that is very simple to use but provides valuable insights into your best qualities (Niemiec 2014, 2018). It extends far beyond the workplace into your family, social, and community life. It has been used by thousands of people worldwide and is a favorite activity among people trying to improve their character strengths awareness and use. You can download the full version at http://www.newharbinger.com/42808.

Learn. Practice. SHARE.

In this chapter, you've learned about different methods, examples, and practices surrounding strengths-spotting. You've explored a range of paths for implementing strengths-spotting in your daily life, which is an important, lifelong skill you can continue to hone and deploy. You've also woven in the strengths-spotting that others can offer you and how you might look at others' observations in relation to your own self-perceptions.

Before moving on, consider this: What is most important for you to take away from this chapter? What is most important to share with others right now?

Consider sharing an insight, a strengths-spotting practice, or a new goal with one person in your life. You might go to the movies with a friend and mutually engage in strengths-spotting of the lead character. You might spot someone's strengths on a social media platform and encourage others to do the same. Explore your "share" below and note with whom you will connect:

_____

_____

_____

_____

_____

CHAPTER 5

Make Strengths Habits to Turn Stress Around

Imagine this:

In every interaction you have with people—day after day, month after month—you spot at least one character strength. You notice your partner's critical thinking ability when he uses logic to analyze a difficult situation you tell him about. You see his social intelligence when he empathizes with your feelings. You see the curiosity in a neighborhood child as she asks you questions about your home and leadership in another child as he organizes a group of kids to play a game. You see kindness in the grocery store clerk as she thoughtfully packs your items. In each of these scenarios, you point out the person's positive quality and express your appreciation for their use of it. You even see strengths in animals, noticing the zest of a dog jumping around while being walked outside and the prudence of a cat that carefully steers away from the dog to its safety. Everywhere you look—on pages and on screens, in the break room and at the dinner table—you are spotting character strengths in each person and each interaction.

And it doesn't stop there. You are also expressing your own strengths in each situation of your life. You use your curiosity, kindness, and social intelligence to ask people about the good things in their lives, give a listening ear when they are suffering, and offer support whenever possible. You use self-regulation and prudence to organize your home and make a positive environment for your family, creativity as you cook interesting and healthy meals, gratitude as you offer heartfelt thanks at the end of each day, teamwork as you collaborate with your partner to handle stress and conflicts together. You are conscious of these character strengths, bringing them forth deliberately and with purpose throughout each day.

You do all of this imperfectly, as best you can. You realize that this strengths work is an ongoing process that evolves and deepens over time.

In this scenario, you are expressing, spotting, and discussing a wide range of positive human qualities. Noticing and using character strengths have become habits. But it's more than simply a strengths routine. You have unleashed strengths in yourself and in the world. You have become these strengths. You *are* curiosity and kindness and gratitude.

Your Habits: Who You Are Is What You Repeatedly Do

Read this again once or twice: Who you are is what you repeatedly do. Let that thought really sink in. In your own life, what do you spend your time doing? Are you a professional television watcher or a person who tries to help others as much as possible? If the latter, then your actions speak to who you are (kind). How do you respond when you get hit hard by stress? Do you get angry, frustrated, and blame others? Or do you call upon your perspective to see the bigger picture of the stress and feel thankful for the opportunity to grow that it allows you? If so, your actions speak to you being a wise and grateful person. Our patterns of behavior reflect who we are.

For me, whenever I think of this philosophical idea of our repeated actions defining who we are, it serves as a wake-up call. I can "repeatedly do" strengths. It hits me like a ton of bricks that it is my actions in life that matter most. What I spend my time worrying about or thinking about does not matter as much as what I do. It's how I treat people, how I initiate, how I spend my time with people. It's my actions that count. It's my actions that tell others who I am. I cannot be perfectly kind or creative, but I can repeatedly move in the direction of those strengths.

These observations bring me to realize that strength, virtue, and goodness are all within our reach. They are trainable. With practice, good habits can be created (just like bad habits are). You can practice gratitude, teamwork, perseverance, and curiosity. You can make them stronger. Research studies show that when you play to your strengths (that is, make them stronger), your stress management and coping improve (Harzer and Ruch 2015; Wood et al. 2011).

The key is to prioritize your strengths. You can commit to learning and growing your strengths—using them when your child is crying, when your partner is complaining, and when your boss ignores your good work. You can bring forth your strengths in a wide range of ways, like calling on your bravery when someone is unhappy with you. Or expressing perseverance to endure an extended period of stress or self-regulation to calm yourself and let it go. Each character strength is highly versatile and packed with potential. With greater understanding and regular practice, your strengths habits will grow.

This chapter will focus on making room for habits to grow, but also on tapping into research-based ways to create strength behaviors throughout your day. You'll practice by weaving strengths into your typical routine. You'll start your day strong by priming your strengths for upcoming stressors, then you'll work on increasing your versatility with strengths use by applying some unique practices, and finally you'll end your day on solid footing with a gratitude practice. After you've had a chance to experiment with some of these strengths practices, you'll have a better idea of a plan you might set forth. We'll conclude by looking at the essential elements of making a strengths plan, including setting intentions, enlisting support, and discovering new ways to receive positive reinforcement for strengths use.

Strong Beginnings: Tune Your Day to Strengths Use

It's a truism to say that breakfast is the most important way to start the day. There's no doubt it gets your metabolism running and your energy up, which can have a helpful effect on stress. But think about these questions:

- What if you could start your day with a more direct effect on stress?

- What if you attached character strengths to your morning routine?

- How would it feel to know that your biggest stressor of the day was under control?

While you're eating your breakfast, you can think ahead to managing your stressors. Then, with confidence that you'll be tackling your stress, you can let go of the extra worries and tensions and focus on enjoying your day.

Here's a bit of background on an approach to try. A group of counselors was asked to think about their clients' best strengths for a few minutes just before they counseled them. For example, one counselor thought about the client as very loving and kind, another recalled a story the client had told the previous week of how they'd used perseverance and bravery to help a stranger they didn't know, and yet another thought about the client's creative use of wordplay and humor. This group was compared with a group of counselors who simply did their counseling as usual, not thinking about client strengths first. The researchers examined what happened, including the potential impact of this approach. The results of this study showed that the clients who received counseling from counselors who thought about their strengths ahead of time benefited in a number of ways over the other group—namely, they made more progress in their counseling session, experienced higher activation of strengths and a greater sense of accomplishment in the session, and enjoyed a stronger relationship with their counselor. This approach of thinking about strengths first is known as *resource priming* (Fluckiger and Grosse Holtforth 2008; Fluckiger et al. 2009).

There's a lot of wisdom in this study. It tells us that there is an advantage to setting ourselves up for success with our strengths. If you think about your strengths, you can quickly create intentions—and a will—for action. You begin to see more clearly that your strengths can turn stress around, and when you're acting from strength, you increase your chances of success.

You can apply this approach by looking ahead in your day—to the to-do list you have to complete, the errands you need to run, the meetings you have to attend, the places you have to take your kids, the demands your supervisor might place on you, and the people you'll likely encounter. You can consider the challenges of each before you even encounter them: Who might be most difficult to interact with? At what point might your anxiety rise? What situations could elicit your frustration? As you choose one potential stressor, your mind is likely already imagining details, conversations, scenarios. But it's unlikely that your mind is automatically playing out the multiple ways your character strengths can be used to handle or overcome the stressor or even thrive within it. You can practice directing your mind to take that approach!

Use Strengths Priming to Prepare for Stressors

To establish resource priming as part of your regular strengths practice, download this worksheet at http://www.newharbinger.com/42808 and fill it out daily.

Name an upcoming stressful event, difficult conversation, or problem you will likely be facing today:

_____

_____

_____

Think about your signature strengths. How might you use them with this stressor? Play out your strengths use in your mind. What specifically will that action look like?

_____

_____

_____

When it comes to the time in your day when this situation is about to occur, don't forget to first prime yourself with your strengths. What might you do to help you remember to reflect on your signature strengths for about five minutes prior? Do you need to set an alarm on your phone? Give yourself a bit of extra time for preparation? What will best help you?

_____

_____

_____

Now that you've started your morning off thinking about your strengths and how they can help you handle some of the stress of your day, let's enhance the versatility of your strengths so you'll be ready to turn to them at any moment.

Getting Versatile with Your Strengths

To see the full force of your strengths, you need to get comfortable working with all 24 of them. We'll examine how each character strength is quite dynamic as you practice very different ways of expressing it—toward other people and toward yourself.

To start, consider these two scenarios:

Scenario 1: Andy took a class on strengths and noticed he is high in honesty. He says: "I use my honesty strength regularly in my life. This mainly comes across by telling people the truth when they ask me questions. Sometimes the truth is difficult for people to hear, but I share it anyway."

Scenario 2: Nolan took a class on strengths and noticed he is high in honesty. He says: "Being honest is who I am. It is part of everything I do. It drives my interactions with family, friends, and coworkers. People always know where I stand on a problem, a social issue, or a burning question because I am clear and direct with my feedback and opinions. I tell it how I see it. I work hard on being honest with myself too. I cherish others' honest feedback about me and my behavior. I try to sift through my biases and stereotypes—to really see myself as clearly as possible. I know it's a lifelong journey, but for me, that's an essential part of it. I also try to live my life in an honest way, with integrity. If you had cameras up in all the rooms of my house and watched my interactions with my wife and kids behind closed doors, you would see the same thing there as you would when I'm out at a restaurant or at a park. I am who I am. I try not to put up a facade. When things get tough, I turn to honesty. When people are sensitive about a topic, I still turn to honesty. When things are going great, I turn to honesty. Some people say that I am too honest, and I simply respond with more honesty! I listen carefully to them and then share with them that I'm striving to find ways to be truthful while also being considerate of their feelings."

Both scenarios show positive strengths use. But Nolan's scenario shows the many ways he uses his signature strength and how important it is to him. It's not just that his explanation is longer, it's that he's tapping into different levels of depth with his strengths use, using it across contexts, with both others and himself, and showing he is open to continuing to grow the strength. As I read Nolan's words, I feel confident that he is not only well versed in his top strength, but that he would likely be quite adaptable and versatile in expressing the strength at times of stress.

This versatility is also seen in each of the 24 character strengths. Each can be used in many different ways and for different purposes. An important general concept that we see in the example of Nolan is that character strengths can be turned inward or outward. In other words, we can focus the strength on another person to help grow that relationship or we can focus the strength on ourselves as we go about our day. Nolan turns his honesty inward in his self-analysis, and he expresses it outwardly in his relationships.

Some of the character strengths are obviously more inward or outward directed; for example, love and gratitude are typically expressed outwardly, while curiosity and creativity are more commonly directed inwardly, when you're alone, exploring a new topic or developing something new.

It can be particularly interesting to do the opposite of what's expected. Kindness is generally viewed as doing something nice for someone. But what happens if you turn your kindness inward and are nice and compassionate to yourself? Or consider forgiveness. What might it look like to be forgiving toward yourself? Likewise, you could take a typically self-directed strength like curiosity and point it toward others; instead of expressing it when you're by yourself searching on the Internet, you could explore a new pathway of group learning, try out a new recipe on your family, or ask a loved one an unexpected question.

The following table shows specific examples of inward and outward expressions of ten character strengths.

Character Strength	Turned Inward	Turned Outward
Creativity	Thinking of three different ways to solve a new personal problem	Reading aloud a short poem you wrote to inspire a loved one
Curiosity	Exploring a new food with all of your senses	Asking a stressed-out colleague a few questions about what energizes them at work
Honesty	Admitting one of your bad habits to yourself	Sharing your true thoughts when someone asks for your opinion
Zest	Going for a walk to revitalize your energy	Expressing enthusiasm and excitement for a loved one when they tell you about something good from their day
Love	Being gentle with yourself in a situation where you are typically judgmental	Offering a warm hug and careful listening to an upset friend
Fairness	Justly deciding to not take on another project to prevent feeling overwhelmed	Giving each of your children the same "dollar amount" of gifts on their birthdays
Forgiveness	Letting go of a mistake you made on a homework assignment	Telling a friend you forgive them after they made a negative comment about you to others
Prudence	Planning out the tasks you will focus on throughout the workday	Mapping out and organizing several back-to-back activities with a friend who is cohosting a party with you
Appreciation of Beauty & Excellence	Reflecting on one of your successful work projects and appreciating the precision and skill you put forth to make it happen	Sharing simple nature photographs on social media for others to marvel at and enjoy
Gratitude	Taking a moment to feel thankful for your life and your level of health in this world	Saying "thank you" to someone in your life for being an important role model

When you consider both the inward and outward expression of one of your strengths, you see your strength in a different way. You expand how you view the strength. This widening perception of your strengths will assist you in managing stress and conflicts over the coming weeks. And it will help you to readily see the potential each strength has.

Your Inward and Outward Strengths Use

Return to your top five signature strengths. Expand your thinking about these strengths by brainstorming how each might be used inwardly and outwardly. Come up with at least one example for each. Remember, inward expressions most often occur when you are by yourself, and outward expressions most often occur when you are in communication with one or more people. You can also think of inward and outward expressions like this: How do you use the signature strength to benefit yourself? How do you use the signature strength to benefit others?

Signature strength #1: _____

Example(s) of expressing it inwardly: _____

_____

_____

_____

Example(s) of expressing it outwardly: _____

_____

_____

_____

Signature strength #2:_____

Example(s) of expressing it inwardly: _____

_____

_____

_____

Example(s) of expressing it outwardly: _____

_____

_____

_____

Signature strength #3: _____

Example(s) of expressing it inwardly: _____

_____

_____

_____

Example(s) of expressing it outwardly: _____

_____

_____

_____

Signature strength #4: _____

Example(s) of expressing it inwardly: _____

_____

_____

_____

Example(s) of expressing it outwardly: _____

_____

_____

_____

Signature strength #5: _____

Example(s) of expressing it inwardly: _____

_____

_____

_____

Example(s) of expressing it outwardly: _____

_____

_____

_____

When you are feeling upset, calling to mind the direction in which you are pointing your strengths can be a pleasant surprise and an immediately calming tool. And if you're interested in even more ways to apply versatility to your strengths use, go to http://www.newharbinger.com/42808 for another activity that will get you used to incorporating them throughout your day: faking your strengths use until you become more comfortable with it as a genuine expression of your authentic self.

Okay, you started your day strong and were flexible and versatile with strengths in the middle part of your day, so now it's time for a strong ending!

Ending Your Day with Strengths

At the end of a stressful day, we often want to put it behind us and simply forget about it. But you can take a different approach, even when your day was loaded with stress, upsetting emotions, and body tension. Although that stress is a reality, another part of that reality is that there were a multitude of good things going on during your day as well. These are usually so overshadowed by the stressors, however, that we forget that the positives are always there.

I therefore encourage you to "tend to the end." Pay attention to the end of your day by pausing to appreciate the fullness of your day.

Over and over, research studies have shown that reflecting at the end of your day on the good things that happened—in many cases, at least three—is linked with an increase in longer-term happiness and a decrease in depression (Gander et al. 2013; Seligman et al. 2005).

This activity, commonly known as "counting your blessings," is a strategy for boosting the strength of gratitude. Gratitude is a connection lubricant. On a basic level, it completes a relationship transaction—you did something nice for me, and I am acknowledging that and showing appreciation. On a deeper level, when offered with genuineness, gratitude enhances our connection with the world, ourselves, and others.

For your strengths practice, download this worksheet at http://www.newharbinger.com/42808 and try a gratitude practice for one week. Each night that week, look back on your day and make note of the good things that occurred and why they seemed to occur. Here are a few pointers: be specific with each example and get into the nuances of the situation or the interaction you had. This is more powerful than simply noting, *I'm grateful for my health, my family, and my friends*—that doesn't say much about who you are. Also, try not to repeat yourself during the week; come up with new, specific examples each day. And if you're motivated to do this for longer than one week, then certainly do so!

Day of the Week	Three Blessings or Good Things	How Each Good Thing Came About	What Character Strengths Did You (or Others) Use?
Sample	1. My spouse rubbed my back for a few minutes this morning before work. 2. A stranger held the door for me as I was entering the building. 3. When I got home from work, one of my kids came running up to me and gave me a big hug.	1. I was feeling worried about my busy day, and my spouse understood this and felt my tense shoulders so rubbed them for me. 2. She must have noticed I was struggling to carry the large box and went out of her way to help me. 3. When I arrived, I yelled out, "I'm home" and I smiled at my kids. This prompted their enthusiasm, which I really appreciated after a long day.	1. It seemed to cause me to experience self-regulation. I felt in control of my emotions. 2. I saw kindness in that person. I felt the urge to be kind shortly after that, and I noticed I was extra nice and caring toward my receptionist. 3. Love. I felt loved and expressed warmth and love through touch.
Day 1	1. 2. 3.	1. 2. 3.	1. 2. 3.
Day 2	1. 2. 3.	1. 2. 3.	1. 2. 3.
Day 3	1. 2. 3.	1. 2. 3.	1. 2. 3.

Day 4	1.	1.	1.
	2.	2.	2.
	3.	3.	3.
Day 5	1.	1.	1.
	2.	2.	2.
	3.	3.	3.
Day 6	1.	1.	1.
	2.	2.	2.
	3.	3.	3.
Day 7	1.	1.	1.
	2.	2.	2.
	3.	3.	3.

As you practice bringing attention to gratitude (and your other character strengths), it expands. Imagine if you practiced this routinely every day for a whole year. You would have noticed and tapped into your gratitude strength over a thousand times! That would be a solid and strong habit.

Review Your Day of Strengths

Now take a moment to look at your strengths practices as they've unfolded from the beginning of your day to the end. Get a closer look at what stands out by answering the questions that follow.

How did your day go? What was it like to bring strengths to the beginning, middle, and end of your day?

_____

_____

_____

_____

Which character strengths seemed most energizing? Most essential for you? How did you express them?

_____

_____

_____

_____

What strengths practices stood out to you? Keep these in mind as you move on to the next section on setting up a specific strengths plan.

_____

_____

_____

Strengths Planning for Your Positive Habit

Now that you've gotten a chance to experiment with some strengths practices throughout your day, you might be feeling energized to make a strengths plan.

Your positive habit is far more likely to be successful if you keep some research-backed tips in mind as you make your plan: (1) set your intention, or goal, and list the obstacles that might get in the way; (2) enlist the support of others; and (3) set up a positive reinforcement loop.

Name Your Strength Intention and Foresee the Challenges

What is the positive habit you would like to set as a regular part of your life? When deciding, you might find it helpful to learn what happened with Cal, a business executive in his thirties, who was very excited to discover all of his signature strengths. So he decided to set one new goal for each strength, and he began taking action immediately with all of them. Things went pretty well at first, but after about one week, Cal's stress at work began to get to him and the five strengths goals he was trying to implement became a burden. He gave them all up. He did nothing with strengths for a while. A few months later, Cal returned to review his strengths goals. His excitement reignited, but this time, he decided to focus on boosting only one signature strength. He set a plan and kept to it for over a year. It was a strong habit. He attributed his success to having a laser focus on his goal, planning ahead with it, and being able to get his head around the potential barriers to the goal.

Research studies support what Cal discovered: too much focus on doing good can backfire. In one study, groups of people who were asked to plan around one virtuous goal were more successful than those who focused on and planned around six virtuous goals (Dalton and Spiller 2012).

Researchers have also discovered you are more likely to make your goal or your strength intention a reality if you name the obstacles that might get in the way and how you will handle them if they do (Gollwitzer and Oettingen 2013; Hudson and Fraley 2015). This technique is sometimes called the *if-then strategy*, where the "if" is the challenge you might encounter and the "then" is how you will confront that challenge successfully.

Take a look at the if-then statements Sandi used for her strength intention to count her blessings each night. She knew one of her likely obstacles was being too tired and therefore less motivated to follow through. She also knew she might forget to do the activity. Here's what Sandi came up with:

If I feel too tired at night to do my gratitude journal, *then* I will use my zest strength and complete it standing up before bed.

If I forget to do the activity one day, *then* the next day I will use my prudence strength to program the alarm on my smartphone to remind me to count my blessings at a specific time each evening.

Try it out yourself.

Set one strength intention or goal that you'd like to take action with each day:

_____

_____

Name two obstacles that might get in the way of your successful strengths action each day. Follow these with your personal if-then strategies.

Obstacle: _____

If-then strategy: _____

_____

_____

Obstacle: _____

If-then strategy: _____

_____

_____

Once you feel comfortable with your new strengths intention—this might take a few weeks—you can then repeat the process with another strengths goal.

Rediscover Your Support Network

Getting support from and connecting with others about your character strengths is a central theme running through this workbook. At the end of each chapter, you're encouraged to connect with others in some way to keep up with your strengths growth. In chapter 3, one of the central behaviors for working with strengths was the second "A" in ROAD-MAP, for "ask." And in the last chapter, you solicited new views of your character strengths with the online Character Strengths 360° tool. Here, we will turn directly to support as a key component of building and keeping up a good habit. Support for our strengths habits comes in many forms, and when it comes to the people in your life who can help you on your journey, there are three types: joiners, cheerleaders, and connectors.

JOINERS

Joiners are people who want to jump in with you when you're doing growth work. They get excited at the prospect of improving themselves and developing new insights and are intrigued by the substance and perceived benefits of working on their strengths. Oftentimes, it's a spouse, significant other, or close friend who's eager to "play around" with strengths with you.

Who will join you in your strengths practice? Who in your life is most curious and zestful when it comes to personal growth? Who's eager to jump in and try something new?

_____

_____

_____

Will you ask them to join you? When will you share your strengths plan with them?

_____

_____

_____

CHEERLEADERS

Cheerleaders don't play in the actual game, but they are a constant support, offering encouragement, giving a burst of energy, and cheering and dancing when the team does well. Cheerleaders err on the side of lifting others up. Perhaps there's someone in your life who is consistently on the sidelines supporting you—a doctor, a coach, a family member, a neighbor, or even your mail carrier? If they're willing to be your cheerleader, you could help them with one of their own goals in return. Ideally, you'll want to become your own best cheerleader, empowering yourself with your strengths; nevertheless, we all need someone rooting us on from the sidelines from time to time.

Who are your cheerleaders? Who will take it upon themselves to check in with you to push you forward in your plan? Who will give you direct encouragement and positive support?

_____

_____

_____

Will you ask them to cheerlead for you? When will you share your strengths plan with them?

_____

_____

_____

CONNECTORS

Connectors are people in your life who don't intend to do an activity with you like joiners, and they won't initiate or push you forward like cheerleaders, but they are happy to lend a listening ear when you bring up self-improvement topics. A connector might be your coffee shop friend, your bowling league buddy, your sibling, or a coworker. Even though they're not working on their own strengths directly, they also don't roll their eyes when you want to talk to them about your signature strengths. They are glad to be the subject of your strengths-spotting, and their social intelligence leads to effective dialogue with you about your plan.

Who are your connectors? Who can you regularly talk to about your strengths growth? Who do you have meaningful conversations with in your life?

_____

_____

_____

Will you ask them to support you? When will you share your strengths plan with them?

_____

_____

_____

Having good, positive relationships is one of the most important avenues for greater well-being in life. Your support system for your strengths work is an integral part of this. Keep your supports at the top of your mind. Support them in kind. And when a supportive person in your life fades away for one reason or another, be sure to connect with others who can help you reach your goals!

Reinforce Your Strengths with a Positive Loop

Studies of the brain and how it works have advanced exponentially in the last couple of decades. Among the findings emerging is a practical one on how habits are formed through cues and reinforced through rewards (Duhigg 2012). Michelle McQuaid, an educator from Australia, has woven strengths into this science of setting up habits and found that, across thousands of people, they can be taught to set up strength habits and then benefit in terms of flourishing, strengths use, setting goals, and feeling more energized (McQuaid and Lawn 2014; McQuaid and VIA Institute 2015). Most of our habits—some good, some not so good—are created automatically, beyond our conscious awareness.

Making a small change in your behavior sounds easy, but many of us are so overwhelmed that we lack the daily mental space and energy to start. The following three-part process can give you that extra push by helping you make your strengths habit more automatic:

Cue: Choose a brief cue, personal prompt, or reminder to get yourself started.

Strength routine: Set a short routine in which you express the character strength. This is the behavioral pattern you want in your life.

Reinforcement: Give yourself some kind of encouragement, positive feedback, pleasurable activity, or permission to do a short activity you are motivated to do as a reward for practicing the habit.

Examples:

Cue: Turn on my computer to start the day.

Strength routine: The cue prompts me to write out a resource priming strategy for the day (how I will respond with my strengths to the event that is most likely to elevate my stress today).

Reinforcement: Take my first sip of freshly brewed coffee.

Cue: Walking by the blue chair in my living room in the morning.

Strength routine: This will remind me to sit in the chair and turn my strength of kindness inward by practicing a loving-kindness meditation for three minutes.

Reinforcement: Play a one-minute game on my smartphone.

YOUR POSITIVE FEEDBACK LOOP

What will be the three-step daily process you apply to your chosen character strengths practice?

Character strength or strengths practice: _____

Cue: _____

Strength routine: _____

_____

Reinforcement: _____

It can be helpful to make small adjustments to any of these three steps in order to keep the habit loop strong. If you have trouble with a certain cue, don't like the strengths routine, or are not feeling the "pull" of the reinforcement you selected, then change it. Make changes until you feel comfortable with and energized by your process.

Learn. Practice. SHARE.

Remember, you are what you repeatedly do. You are well on your way to implementing sustainable habits so that your actions in life (what you repeatedly do) are your strengths. In this chapter, you've taken a new approach to your day. You've gotten ahead of stress, preempting its impact by using your strengths and starting off your day strong. You've become more versatile with your strengths use as you turn them inward and outward more readily, and you've ended your day in a strong way with a potent gratitude practice. You then set a specific strengths intention and used a number of powerful tools (if-then strategies, support system planning, and positive feedback loops) to make your strengths habit a success.

Before we move on to the second part of this workbook, reflect on this: What is your biggest takeaway from this chapter? What is most important for you to share with others right now?

_____

_____

_____

_____

_____

_____

_____

Midway Review: What Are Your Stress Levels?

It's time to reassess your stress levels! Recall the table at the beginning of chapter 1 in which you listed ten to fifteen situations in your life that brought you some level of stress and then you rated the intensity of your stress on a scale from 1 to 10.

Turn back to that table now and take a fresh look at each situation. In the second column ("Mid"), record your current intensity level for each. If the situation is no longer an issue, you can give it a 0. This reassessment is important because changes in our stress—how we perceive it and how we manage it—can be subtle. Looking at different situations across separate time points can offer you wider perspective and insight.

Do you notice any patterns across the stressors? Big changes, little changes, increases, decreases? As you look at the situations and the changes (or lack thereof) in stress intensity, is there anything noteworthy (for example, the work stressors stayed the same, the more personal stressors decreased, those involving people had a small dip)? Explore your reactions here:

_____

_____

_____

_____

_____

_____

PART TWO

Ways Strengths Can Boost Your Daily Resourcefulness

CHAPTER 6

Apply Strengths to Work and Health

For thousands of years, philosophers, theologians, and scientists have used various phrases and terms in an attempt to describe how humans might best express their goodness and their virtues—phrases like these:

- The golden mean

- The middle way

- The doctrine of the mean

- The Goldilocks principle

- Optimal strengths use

Whether it's Aristotle, the Buddha, Confucius, fairy-tale authors, or modern researchers, their message is the same: there must be balance in our use of strengths.

Consider any good quality, virtue, or strength, and you can view its expression as occurring on a continuum. You can have too much of a good thing. Too much love of learning, and you might be acting like a know-it-all; too much leadership, and you're acting like an authoritarian; too much judgment, and you're probably viewed as cynical or narrow-minded. These are examples of *strengths overuse*. You can also express too little of a good thing (or none at all) in a situation. You might express very little creativity in a new social group, so people might see you as bored or unimaginative. Too little kindness is often viewed as selfishness, while too little bravery is typically seen as cowardice or fearfulness. These are examples of *strengths underuse*.

There is usually no precise recipe for the balance between overuse and underuse. It is often a matter of interpretation based on the demands of the situation and the people in it.

For example, let's say you wanted to express your curiosity strength to different people by asking them questions. You decide to ask the same three questions (in the same tone of voice) to a close friend at home, a coworker in the break room, and a stranger walking down the street. Then you ask each of them whether they thought you were overusing your curiosity with these questions, underusing it, or whether it was "just right." Your friend, who is used to your questions, might say it was just right and typical for you. Your coworker's response might be that you were overusing your curiosity because they felt intruded upon and it seemed that you were being nosey about their personal business. Meanwhile, the stranger might think you underused your curiosity because they wanted to connect more and wanted you to challenge them further with your questions. Moreover, the same three people may judge your use differently in different scenarios—say, at a funeral home, a sporting event, or in a restaurant. Your curiosity remains equal in terms of both the questions posed and your tone of voice, but the situation and the people can change. This is where overuse and underuse emerge.

And then there's *optimal strengths use.* This refers to strengths expression that is strong, shows mindful attentiveness to yourself and others, and is balanced and sensitive to the particular situation. Optimal strengths use has been found in research to be connected with greater flourishing and life satisfaction and less depression, whereas overuse and underuse have each been associated with higher depression and less flourishing and life satisfaction (Freidlin, Littman-Ovadia, and Niemiec 2017). Referred to by Aristotle as the "golden mean," optimal use means to use the right amount of a strength in the right context. Optimal use of a strength always—because of its strong and balanced nature—brings along other character strengths to the situation. Think of a time when you and a friend were brainstorming ideas about how to spend your evening. You were expressing your creativity by coming up with many ways to have fun, yet you were also likely open-minded (judgment) and interested (curiosity) in what your friend's ideas were as well. This flexibility kept you from overusing your creativity in this situation.

Each of the 24 character strengths can be plotted along a continuum of degrees, where the center represents optimal strengths use for a given situation. As you express higher levels of a strength, there comes a point when it is being overplayed, when it's too strong for the environment or the people around you—like when your energy and zest become annoying or overactive. On the flip side, you can bring less and less of a strength to a situation to the extent that it becomes too little for the people around you—like when you're not displaying much perseverance on a project, such that you appear unproductive or lazy to others.

Continuum for Overuse, Underuse, and Optimal Use of Character Strengths

This figure can serve as a mental template when you're approaching any situation. Ask yourself which strength you might use, how much of that strength would be best, and how you can prevent both overuse and underuse of it.

Finding Your Optimal Use

Let's explore your own "golden mean" on the continuum of your strengths use.

Start by choosing one of your signature strengths that you'd like to take a closer look at:

_____

How does this strength come across when you are using it well? Give an example of when you felt good about the use of the strength and when others seemed to respond positively to this use:

_____

_____

_____

Now provide an example of when you overused this strength and it caused you or others stress. Include details about how you brought the strength forward too strongly. What was the reaction of others?

_____

_____

_____

_____

What will help you better manage this overuse in the future? Do you need to dial down the strength use a bit? Call upon another strength to temper it?

_____

_____

_____

Even when something's a signature strength, you can still underuse it (some people underuse their signature strengths quite a bit in life). Give an example of when you underused the strength you've been exploring, in a way that caused you or others stress. What was going on in the situation—or within you—that contributed to you not deploying enough of this strength?

_____

_____

_____

To help with underuse, what might you do to elevate this strength more in the future? Will you need to empower yourself by practicing with the strength ahead of time? Might you remind yourself that you have this strength to turn to within you?

_____

_____

_____

We will use these ideas of striving toward balance between strengths overuse and underuse—finding your golden mean or optimal use—as we explore the application of character strengths in two specific areas: your work and your health.

Strengths Use at Work

Do you get bored at work? When you're working on a project or daily task, do you feel disengaged, disinterested, or distracted? Ever find yourself watching the clock, eager for your next break or day's end?

If so, then a good next question to ask yourself is: *What character strength(s) am I underusing?*

When we bring forth the best parts of ourselves, we feel more energy, happiness, and connection with what we are doing. If you are disconnected from what you are doing, you may be in a state of stress, in need of strengths use. Although increasing strengths use at work will not always be the answer for every stressor, it is a straightforward approach to turn to when you experience tension, boredom, or apathy.

We spend an abundance of hours of our life at our job, so it's important we make the most of that time. I remember working on an assembly line at a beer distributing and recycling plant more than twenty years ago. Although assembly work is usually considered especially boring, I don't recall feeling that way on the job; on the contrary, generally speaking, I felt interested and engaged. I chalk this up to my signature strength of curiosity. I was curious about the bottle labels, I enjoyed scouting the factory for new marketing materials or trinkets the distributors and truck drivers brought in, I was attentive to the various sounds of the plant, and I was intrigued by the machines that crushed the cans and bottles. While I sorted the colored bottles, I explored. While I mashed cans, I listened. Boredom was not an issue because my curiosity was ever-present.

Someone else working on an assembly line might turn to their own signature strength of social intelligence as they interact with the other workers, or to their appreciation of excellence as they marvel at the precision of the machinery and how the whole process comes together as an organized system.

You can align your signature strengths with your job regardless of what your work is. A teacher might turn to her top strengths of zest and hope to engage the students. A construction foreman can turn to his leadership and prudence as he follows a specific plan and manages a crew. An accountant might wonder how her highest strength of love relates to her profession, but upon reflection, she realizes that she loves working with numbers and mathematical formulas, that she treats all her coworkers with warmth, and that she's consistently thoughtful to her boss by submitting her forms to him early each day to ease his pressure.

One set of researchers put this concept of aligning work tasks and strengths to the test (Harzer and Ruch 2016). They randomly selected workers to use four of their signature strengths during work tasks for the period of a month. Compared to a control group, the workers who aligned their strengths at work had higher life satisfaction and greater levels of thinking of their work as a "calling." This belief makes the work feel especially meaningful, like an extension of self. The study also highlights that it's particularly important for workers to know and use their signature strengths—it doesn't matter which of the 24 is highest, it only matters that the person is aware of using their signature strengths.

Why not turn to your most energizing qualities—give your worklife a strengths workout?

Align Your Strengths with Work Activities

Consider the five tasks or activities that you do most frequently at work (attending meetings, emailing clients, making sales calls, writing reports). Now consider your top five character strengths. Using the examples as a model, come up with at least one way you can bring one or more of your strengths to each of the five tasks. This activity also asks you to consider how you might overuse and underuse your strengths to help you prevent imbalances and stay in the zone of optimal use. You can complete the worksheet here and download it for additional practice at http://www.newharbinger.com/42808 to start taking action at work!

Work Task/ Activity	Signature Strength	Alignment (how you will use the strength while doing the task)	What might overuse look like?	What might underuse look like?
Running a meeting	Humor Gratitude	I will tell a funny story to start off the meeting. I will spot one coworker's strength at each meeting and express my appreciation to them.	Telling two or three jokes in a row that take up too much time. Becoming too gushy with my gratitude and losing focus on why I'm doing it.	Not laughing at a colleague's joke or funny story. Forgetting to spot strengths of my coworkers.
Storing medical files	Prudence	When I have a stack of files, I will find a way to organize them in smaller stacks and put them away in groups in a timely way.	If this approach to organizing takes up more time than it saves me.	Seeing files stack up day after day and avoiding filing them.

Work Task/ Activity	Signature Strength	Alignment (how you will use the strength while doing the task)	What might overuse look like?	What might underuse look like?
1				
2				
3				
4				
5				

Now that you've found expression of yourself in your daily work activities, let's expand this to others in your workplace. Take a moment to consider each of your main coworkers. What are their signature strengths? What strengths do they bring forth strongly in the workplace? What do you most appreciate or admire about each person? Be sure to include your teammates, subordinates/supervisees, and especially your boss/supervisor. Start with the colleagues you work most closely with, then you can add more people if you wish.

Person	What do you appreciate most in this person? (two of their top character strengths)	How do you see these top strengths in this person? (give a brief example)
Boss/ Supervisor		
Coworker		
Coworker		
Coworker		
Coworker		
Coworker		

You're off and running in deploying character strengths in different ways to energize your work and appreciate others. Now let's shift gears and turn to another important area of your life.

Strengths Use with Your Health

In chapter 1, we talked about health as one of the primary areas of well-being. It's a central element of flourishing, and it equates to feeling alive and vital, strong in body and mind.

You can create positive health habits no matter what your status is, whether you struggle with a chronic disease, are overweight, or have no health problems. You can activate improved health by turning to what I call the "five pillars of health" in your lifestyle:

1. **Exercise:** following a regular exercise plan and a schedule for movement/walking to increase your activity and motion, like steps taken per day.

2. **Sleep:** getting quality, uninterrupted sleep daily, usually seven to nine hours per night, to feel generally refreshed upon awakening.

3. **Eating:** consuming a healthy diet high in fruits and vegetables, along with other essential nutrients, accompanied by managing the intake of unhealthy foods (such as white sugar, white flour, fast food).

4. **Social Activity:** having a regular outlet for your social life with friends, family, and community, such as volunteering and engaging in a spiritual group, to enrich your life meaning.

5. **Self-Regulation:** engaging in a regular practice of calming, focusing, connecting, or strengths-boosting to take care of and regulate yourself (examples include relaxation techniques, mindfulness, transcendental meditation, centering prayer, religious ritual, loving-kindness meditation, self-hypnosis, and biofeedback).

In working with countless clients on their health, I have seen attention to these five pillars lead them to improve their quality of life, prioritize their health, find balance, overcome problems, and empower them to cope with their stress. And while each of these pillars has been written about extensively, I will focus here on a relatively untapped area relating to them: the use of character strengths to enhance and support each. Indeed, character strengths form the foundation of them and can hardly be separated from them. How can you do volunteer work, for example, without teamwork and kindness? How can you commit to a full night's sleep every day without prudence?

Character Strengths and the Five Pillars of Health

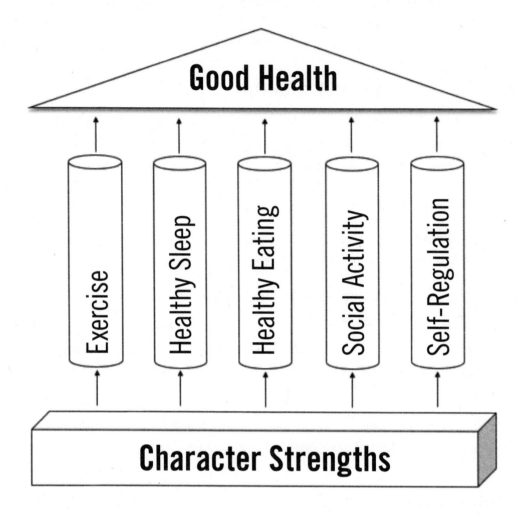

Although research on character strengths applied to health remains a newer area of study, it's expanding each year and shows promise (Niemiec and Yarova 2018). In one study, all 24 strengths (except for humility and spirituality) were connected with multiple health behaviors, including an active lifestyle, proper diet, and cardiorespiratory fitness (Proyer et al. 2013). And certain character strengths have been shown to have a particularly strong connection with good physical health, such as gratitude (Emmons and McCullough 2003), zest (Ryan and Frederick 1997), and self-regulation (Proyer et al. 2013).

In many cases, health improvement comes down to one thing: behavior activation. As much as health gurus will tout certain regimens as magic and special approaches as necessary for improvement, the one thing that must be done is activating your behavior. In fact, behavioral activation is one of the most established interventions in all of psychology, shown to be consistently useful in lowering depression and increasing well-being in study after study (Mazzucchelli, Kane, and Rees 2010).

But behavior activation doesn't have to be intimidating. Often, one small change can make a big difference. If starting to exercise seems overwhelming, buy a cheap pedometer and just start tracking your steps. If you regularly eat out at fast-food restaurants three times per week, cut it down to once. If meeting people socially causes anxiety for you, start with social media interactions. When you make one small change toward better health, you are likely to feel empowered and more likely to make a second small change.

In terms of your own health, no doubt there are areas that could use improvement, but let's start off by reflecting on what is already strong for you. Maybe you go to bed at the same time each night or eat several servings of fruit each day. Maybe it's part of your routine to connect with friends each week by phone or during outings. It's likely you are particularly strong in one or more of the five pillars.

What regular, positive health habits do you already engage in?

_____

_____

_____

_____

Choosing just one of these good habits, which character strengths are you using with it? How are you using the strength(s) in an optimal way (without overusing)?

_____

_____

_____

_____

Which pillar of health needs improvement in your life?

_____

Why did you choose this area? What is motivating you to attend to it?

_____

_____

_____

_____

You've probably tried a variety of techniques to improve this area in the past. Experiment with something different. Look to your character strengths. What character strengths are you overusing and underusing in this area? Not enough self-kindness when you struggle to keep up with an exercise routine? Too much prudence when you spend all your time planning and not actually doing? Or perhaps you are trying to stick with a self-regulation practice but then overuse your critical thinking by being hard on yourself when you forget? Brainstorm your potential underuses and overuses here:

_____

_____

_____

_____

Now look to your signature strengths—your natural sources of energy and motivation. How might you use one or two of your signature strengths to help you fortify this pillar of health? How might a signature strength (or one of your other character strengths) help you stimulate an underused strength or tame an overused strength?

_____

_____

_____

_____

Health is a journey for life. Keep these five pillars of health in mind from month to month. Return to these questions when you are looking for a fresh start or a reboot on one of your health habits.

Learn. Practice. SHARE.

In this chapter, you've explored the application of character strengths within two major domains of your life: work and health. Before moving on to chapter 7, where you'll explore another central life domain (relationships), take stock of your key learnings from this chapter.

What are a couple of the most important insights you had? Are you discovering new ways to align your strengths with your tasks at work? Are you appreciating one of your positive health habits? Which of the pillars of health are you giving more attention to?

It is important to share your insights with others. It's a way to let your family and friends understand the effort you are making to impact your stress and well-being, and it may encourage them to make changes as well. What learnings from this chapter will you share and with whom?

_____

_____

_____

_____

CHAPTER 7

Overcome Stress in Relationships

What is the secret to happiness?

I don't pretend to know the answer, but if I had to bet based on my understanding of the latest psychological science and the wisdom of the ages, I'd say the secret has something to do with cultivating healthy relationships with others. To connect with others in positive ways that contribute to both your well-being and the well-being of the other is a win-win in which each side of the relationship benefits and supports the other.

Researchers have repeatedly found that social relationships play an essential, necessary role in happiness (Caunt et al. 2013; Diener and Oishi 2005). Moreover, not only do good relationships lead to greater happiness, but happiness leads to better relationships (Diener and Seligman 2004). It's a two-way street.

This sounds simple and straightforward, but we are quick to take relationships for granted. The reality is, they are often the source of both our greatest joys and our greatest struggles. Consider these snapshots of stories of a few people:

- Jacob is married to a very supportive and loving woman, which is the source of his greatest gratitude in life. At the same time, his boss is the source of his greatest suffering; he perceives her to be authoritarian, abrupt, and demeaning to him in their interactions. He thinks about this day and night and spends most of the time he has with his wife not cherishing their relationship, but complaining about his boss.

- Throughout Morgan's life, she has been enriched by many close friendships. She has sustained them for decades and spends many weeks per year traveling with her friends and sharing her life with them. Now that she is moving into older age, some of her closest friends are dying. She has lost three in the past year. This has caused her substantial grief and has led to a large decline in her previously abundant social life.

- Laurie is a single mother to a precocious six-year-old son named J.J. This is her closest and most cherished relationship, and her life revolves around him. Laurie finds that her deepest laughter, her highest excitement, and her brightest smiles come when she's with him. J.J. brings out the best in her. She'd also be the first to admit that he brings out other parts of her that she doesn't especially like, such as anger, embarrassment, and anxiety as she tries to parent her sometimes challenging, oppositional, and rambunctious son.

You can view your close relationships like a wave. For much of the time, a wave is not very noticeable, hidden within the vast ocean. Eventually, the wave rises and falls, is predictable and unpredictable, can become serene and turbulent, and can flow steadily and crash chaotically. Each of our most important relationships is like that wave. You can step back and observe the rise and fall of joy, of frustration, and of intensity during interactions, activities, and routines. You can savor and appreciate the steady flow and tranquility, and you can keep a mindful, bigger-picture perspective during the fluctuations and turbulence. Knowing this reality of our close relationships can give you the extra insight and comfort you need during stressful (yet always changing) moments.

The focus of this chapter will be on your close relationships. This most clearly refers to your relationship partner, but you'll find you can also apply this work to your children, other family members, close friends, and coworkers.

A Model for Close Relationships and Character Strengths

Several years ago, my colleague Donna Mayerson and I developed a conceptual model and an online course on character strengths and relationships for the VIA Institute on Character. In this model, we offer a full view on how to think about and use character strengths to develop and sustain close, positive relationships. There are five main elements of the model into which character strengths can be integrated, feeding and uplifting each component to form the foundation for strong and lasting relationships:

1. Knowing and being known to each other

2. Appreciating and accepting the other

3. Nurturing the other

4. Repairing and resolving conflicts

5. Growing together

This model was created based on extensive experience counseling others, on previous and current research on relationships and character strengths, and on external expert opinion.

Although the emphasis is placed on others (knowing them, nurturing them, and so on), this does not mean neglecting oneself, one's own self-care or strengths. Caring for oneself along the entire journey of cultivating positive relationships is crucial. As discussed in chapter 4, much of this work is about "knowing thyself" and appreciating and accepting your own character strengths. The figure below shows the connections between character strengths and each of the five elements in this model.

A Model for Positive Relationships and Character Strengths

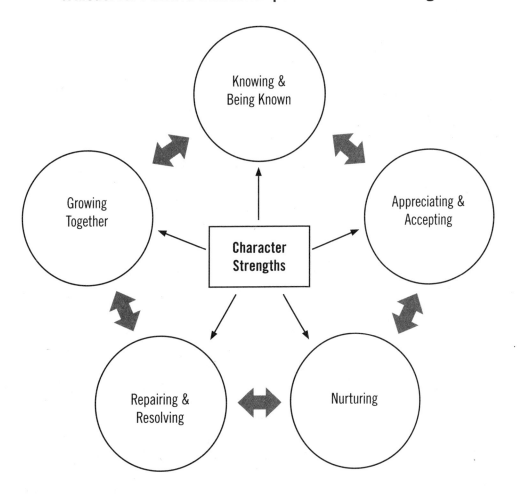

You'll recall from chapter 2 one of my favorite phrases: "All 24 character strengths matter." This is especially true when it comes to the importance of using all the strengths in our closest relationships. I have organized the 24 into four "S" categories to offer a new way of thinking about character strengths in relationships. Though any of the 24 can be argued to fit most of the categories, some seem to lend themselves, generally speaking, into one more than the others.

- **Staples:** For several character strengths, no explanation is needed—the importance of love, kindness, fairness, honesty, and forgiveness to close relationships is obvious. These traditionally "other-oriented" strengths within you are crucial to assisting you in "tending and befriending" others and expressing your "heart." How can you create a good relationship without these central strengths?

- **Sustainers:** Equally straightforward is the need for perseverance, perspective, self-regulation, and social intelligence in *sustaining* any long-term relationship. The energy embedded in zest and the positivity in hope make these strengths sustainers as well. And what about viewing your intimate relationship as a "team"? You and your partner can see yourselves as players on the same team—both on an equal level, jointly working together toward a common goal such as relationship happiness. The strength of teamwork can therefore also be a sustaining quality.

- **Supporting Cast:** But the main ingredients aren't the only ones that matter! Isn't it also helpful to sometimes add the spice of creativity, the curiosity to pose open-ended questions, leadership to take charge of a new activity, humor to offer levity, and a healthy dose of gratitude? How about sticking up for yourself sometimes (with bravery), but not too often (thus using prudence)?

- **Surprises:** Then there are less direct, less obvious ways to add an unexpected positive jolt to your relationship. What new pursuit might you and your partner engage in together to express your love of learning? In what ways can you describe your partner or their behaviors using your appreciation of beauty or excellence? How might you use your judgment/critical thinking in a debate with your partner to see things completely from their side? How can you talk to your partner about your spirituality as a way of expressing meaning and purpose in your life? Can you apply your humility to bring your attention and energy to your partner for an extended period of time?

As you can see, all 24 strengths are important for building, repairing, and maintaining a healthy relationship. A study of married people ranging in age and years of marriage found that all 24 strengths, as well as groupings of those strengths (strengths of the heart, strengths of the mind, intrapersonal and interpersonal strengths), were positively related to marital satisfaction (Guo, Wang, and Liu 2015). Other research reveals a number of benefits reflected in this model. For example, naming and deploying character strengths in one's partner is associated with greater relationship satisfaction (Lavy, Littman-Ovadia, and Bareli 2014), and strengths have been shown to be a central process among same-sex couples (Rostosky and Riggle 2017). In another study, researchers examined hundreds of couples and found that some of the best ways to improve a relationship were to engage in other-focused behavior, to display generosity and kindness to improve and deepen a mutual awareness of each other, and to direct one's own strengths and virtues toward the relationship partner (Veldorale-Brogan, Bradford, and Vail 2010).

Knowing and Being Known

In Zulu, the most common home language in South Africa, the single word *sawubona* (pronounced sow-bone-ah) is a greeting that means "I see you." When an indigenous person in South Africa meets another, they look closely in each other's eyes for ten or fifteen seconds and utter this word. It means more than "hi" or "hello"; it goes much deeper to something akin to "I see who you are, your core qualities, I see your humanity. I respect you." This is precisely what relational character strengths-spotting and sharing is all about. It's about truly recognizing the other person. It's about telling them that you "see" them.

Ngikhona (pronounced gee-ko-nah) is the typical response to *sawubona* in Zulu, meaning "I am here." The speaker is acknowledging the feeling of being recognized and understood.

These two words capture the first element of the positive relationships model—knowing the other person's character strengths and being known by your strengths. Imagine this: you turn to your loved one, look them in the eyes, and say, "I see you." After a few seconds, they respond with, "I am here." At first, there might be some anxiety or awkwardness, but what else would you feel? What would that be like? What if, by this, you were mutually implying that you see each other's best qualities?

Research shows the importance of this. Studies of couples who feel understood during times of conflict experience stronger relationships because this perceived understanding signals that the partners are invested in each other (Gordon and Chen 2016). It might be that feeling understood and known by each other's character strengths helps to manage stress and conflicts by dampening the negative energy or tense emotions. Strengths act like glue in our relationships, connecting us in countless ways.

In numerous workshops I've conducted over the years, I've had couples pair up and rekindle the process of being seen in a very simple way. I invite them to interview each other. I ask them to interview each other about their strengths and how they use them and to share stories about when they felt they were at their best. It is not uncommon for me to hear—both from couples who have been together for decades and from longtime colleagues or close friends—"Wow, after all these years, I didn't know that about you" or "I've always wondered about that quirk you have, and now I see it's based in strength!" The positivity and engagement are palpable. To focus on strengths is to offer a freshness to the relationship. It brings new insight so that each person can begin to "see" the other and to "know" them from a different perspective.

Conduct a Strengths Interview

Select someone with whom you're in a close relationship. Interview them from a strengths perspective. If it feels a bit awkward to do or you don't know how to start, try saying something like this:

I am spending some time focusing on what is strongest in myself and in the people I care about. Part of this is learning to take a strengths-based approach. I would like to practice this by learning more about your best qualities and how they connect with who you are, as well as with your past successes. Would you be willing to explore this with me?

When ready, move into some specific questions, either the following ones to use as a guide or questions you create on your own:

- What are your highest strengths, your signature strengths? (If the person has not taken the VIA Survey, then show them the list of the 24 strengths and have them select a few.)

- Tell me about a recent time when you were at your best or when you felt relly connected. What was that like? What character strengths played a role in this experience?

- What character strengths are most closely linked with your life successes? Which are used most in your relationships?

- When you consider our relationship, what are the elements that make it strong?

- When do you feel most "seen" and appreciated? When do you feel you can really be yourself?

- Which character strengths would you like to use more in our relationship? Which would you like me to use more?

- Tell me about a stressor or difficult situation that you successfully resolved. What character strengths did you use to resolve it?

Who did you interview?

_____

What was it like to take a strengths approach with this person?

_____

_____

_____

What character strengths did you notice and hear (even if not directly named) in their responses?

_____

_____

_____

What did you notice in the person during the interview? Did your questions and your focus on strengths reveal different emotional reactions, new insights, or surprises?

_____

_____

_____

Can you carry some elements of this strengths-based conversation with you when you interact in the future with this person? Can you transfer some insights to your relationships with other people? Identify those elements/insights here:

_____

_____

_____

_____

Appreciating and Accepting

Once we have a deeper sense of who the person is that we're relating to, we come to more fully appreciate them and accept them for who they are. The challenge is to then express this appreciation. How might you convey how much you value this person?

Todd Kashdan, a professor at George Mason University, and his colleagues (2017) found that relationship partners who recognize and appreciate each other's character strengths also experience greater commitment to the relationship and feel their needs are being met (such as the need for belonging and for autonomy). In addition, the couples had greater relationship satisfaction, reported higher sexual satisfaction, and felt their goals in life were being supported. Conversely, they found the opposite to be true as well: relationship dissatisfaction was found to be connected to partners viewing each other's character strengths unfavorably, as having a "cost" attached to them—for example, overuse of strengths or strengths seen to be adversely affecting the other in some way.

Take the Partner Strengths Questionnaire

You can take an abbreviated version of the Kashdan study's Partner Strengths Questionnaire here. This tool was created for intimate relationship partners to explore and appreciate the other's character strengths, but you can use it to examine any of your close relationships.

Name of the person you're assessing with this questionnaire: _____

Name one of the character strengths that most accurately reflects this person. As you think about this person, what is most central to who they are, what lies at their core? The use of what strength seems to energize and excite them?

Character strength #1: _____

Describe a recent situation (that you witnessed or just heard about) in which this person used this strength:

_____

_____

_____

For the rest of the questions about this relationship partner, use the following scale:

Not at all			**Somewhat**			**Extremely**
1	2	3	4	5	6	7

STRENGTH USE AND EFFECTIVENESS

_____ To the best of your knowledge, how often does your partner use this strength in a typical week?

_____ How effective is your partner at using this strength? In other words, how well do they perform activities that rely on this strength?

_____ Total score for use/effectiveness

STRENGTH APPRECIATION

_____ How important is it to you that this person uses this strength?

_____ Do you find yourself more committed to the relationship when you see this person using this strength?

_____ Are you more satisfied with your relationship after seeing this person use this strength?

_____ Total score for appreciation

COSTS OF THE STRENGTH

_____ Does this person's strength end up causing any problems or conflict in your relationship?

_____ How difficult or demanding is it for this person to use this strength?

_____ After using this strength, how drained does this person feel?

_____ Total score for costs

Higher scores on strengths use/effectiveness and strengths appreciation reveal greater understanding and appreciation of this person's character strengths. Be sure to let them know your appreciation! A higher score on strengths costs reflects a greater potential for strengths overuse, which *may* contribute to stress or conflict in the relationship. It's important to mutually explore this with your partner.

Strengths Appreciation in a Close Relationship

Now that you're expanding your awareness of your appreciation and acceptance of the character strengths of someone important in your life, it's time to take some action with that person! You can download this activity at http://www.newharbinger.com/42808 for ongoing use in your strengths practice.

1. Choose one of your close relationships and identify three of the person's best character strengths.

Strength #1: _____

Strength #2: _____

Strength #3: _____

2. Recall a recent incident in which the person admirably displayed each of these strengths. How did you see the strength expressed?

Story for strength #1: _____

_____

_____

Story for strength #2: _____

_____

_____

Story for strength #3: _____

_____

_____

3. Express appreciation. Share with the person what you wrote, explaining why their character strengths use is important to you and valued by you. For example, it may make you feel more emotionally attracted to them, more committed in the relationship, or happier when you are around them. Appreciation can also be expressed nonverbally. How will you express appreciation to this person?

Appreciation for strength #1: _____

_____

_____

Appreciation for strength #2: _____

_____

_____

Appreciation for strength #3: _____

_____

_____

Nurturing

When I was on a weeklong meditation retreat in upstate New York, one of the activities we participated in was mindful speaking and mindful listening within a small group. Each person shared from their experiences whatever they wished to say—the struggles, the positives, and anything in between. When it was my turn, I shared that I was bothered by some of the ways my wife and I interact. The group leader—typically silent and simply allowing each person to talk—turned to me and asked if I've practiced "secret watering." She explained that this meant to "water the seeds" of my wife, without strategy or plan, without needing something in return, and without her knowing that I was following a "technique." In other words, point out and encourage her best qualities, champion her for those qualities, love her for them, and create an environment that allows her to express them. Water her seeds of strength. This has proven to be a productive approach for me and many others who study mindfulness and character strengths (Niemiec 2014).

This is also what is meant by the element of nurturing. As researcher Kelly McGonigal (2015) has explained, the caring and helping of others triggers our "biology" of courage and hope. Our use of compassion opens up other strengths in a deep way.

Nurturing Seeds of Strength in Others

You can practice nurturing strengths in your close relationships with the questions that follow.

Let's start by choosing just one of your close relationships and watering the seeds of that relationship. How might you deliberately encourage this person's strengths? Identify a specific scenario in which you will offer "secret watering." How will you do it?

_____

_____

_____

Now be a detective for the good. Name a situation in which you typically do not spot this person's strengths. How might you use your curiosity and judgment/critical thinking to find a strength or two to point out and reinforce in them?

_____

_____

_____

We should all be careful to not mindlessly react to others' intensities. When others are feeling an intense emotion—anger, anxiety, sadness—that's often when they need nurturance the most.

When others are suffering, how might you respond with compassion?

_____

_____

_____

We should also be champions of others' good news. One of the best ways to nurture others is to notice the uplift in energy when they share something positive that happened to them, such as a gratifying experience at work, a new achievement, or something that made them happy. If you respond to their good news with curious questioning, encouragement, and optimism, that helps them capitalize on the good news and keep that energy flowing, which science tells us is connected with higher well-being for you and them (Gable et al. 2004; Reis et al. 2010).

When someone shares good news with you, how might you respond in an active, curious, and encouraging way?

_____

_____

Another important step in nurturing close relationships is to savor the good—to deliberately try to prolong the positive emotions that are occurring while they are occurring. Savoring has been shown to have extensive scientific benefits in boosting well-being (Bryant and Veroff 2007). One form of savoring is *positive reminiscence,* in which you reflect on a positive experience in one of your close relationships. It's like giving your relationship an emotional multivitamin. This feel-good remembering is a reflection on the specific details of an event, the emotions and sensations that were felt, and the feelings toward each other that resulted.

Practice positive reminiscence here by writing about a fulfilling experience you had with someone close to you. Then read it to the other person and ask them to reminisce as well.

_____

_____

_____

_____

When you nurture your relationship and your partner's strengths, you are creating *virtuous circles*—building a mindful awareness (for you and them) of strengths and cultivating those qualities for future use. Mindful strengths use reinforces itself (Niemiec 2014), so keep spreading those strengths in your relationship!

Repairing and Resolving

Obviously, relationships aren't always rosy with positivity. Problems and conflicts emerge in small and large forms. Some loom for weeks and months in the background like an elephant in the room, and others are poignantly expressed on the face of your loved one.

If you look closely, you might discover that character strengths can act as "hot buttons"—that is, sensitive areas or relationship triggers. This can contribute to or even cause difficulties. For example, have you ever been irritated by your partner's use of too much humor? Overwhelmed by their critical thinking ability in trying to solve a problem? Drowned by their incessant questioning (curiosity) or barrage of ideas (creativity)? When you perceive that your partner is using too much of a strength (insisting on complete fairness in holiday gift giving, for instance) or using too little of a strength (not being very kind to a neighbor who is struggling), then this can fire up your hot button. When you notice yourself getting upset, pause and ask yourself: *Which of my character strengths is being triggered right now?*

When we are upset, character strengths are often the last thing on our mind. But what if they were at the top of your mind?

In some situations, the self-insight that you are being triggered by a strength hot button is all you'll need to help reframe the scenario and take a new look at it. You can then let it go and move on or take action in some way. Other times, further work is needed.

This is where synergies and collisions come in. A *character strengths synergy* occurs when two or more strengths come together and provide a positive benefit; the results show that the sum of the parts is greater than the individual strengths. A *character strengths collision* occurs when two or more strengths collide and bring about stress or conflict; they are worse together than either is alone. Synergies and collisions can occur within ourselves or between ourselves and others, as shown in this four-quadrant model (Niemiec 2018).

Four-Quadrant Model of Character Strengths Synergies and Collisions

Character Strengths	Synergies (1 + 1 = 3)	Collisions (1 + 1 = 0)
Within yourself (intrapersonal)	Teri is a mother whose strengths of fairness and creativity come together strongly as she develops new games and activities and includes her kids' ideas in the process.	Rebecca's interest in collecting research online for a presentation (love of learning) collides with her penchant for watching online videos (curiosity), and the result is procrastination, not getting her work done.
Between yourself and others (interpersonal)	Stacey's bravery in facing the challenge of moving her family to a new city merges well with her husband Scott's prudence in creating a detailed spreadsheet that maps out the costs and benefits of each potential neighborhood; their new home ends up being a great fit for their family.	Brad's perseverance to keep working week after week on a project collides with his teammate Tara's strength of perspective, as she keeps insisting the project cannot be completed and should therefore be abandoned before more costs build up.

Let's bring these concepts of hot buttons, synergies, and collisions together and explore them in an activity.

Transforming Relationship Stress with Strength Reframes

Name a topic or situation that comes up in one of your relationships that triggers you—something that gets you off balance or upsets you:

_____

_____

_____

_____

What character strength is being triggered in you? Why?

_____

_____

_____

_____

Now that you've built some new insight on this hot-button issue, what might you do different next time? What character strengths could you use to temper what was triggered?

_____

_____

_____

_____

To dig a bit deeper, consider if there is a "strengths collision" at play. In other words, are there two strengths (in yourself or between you and your partner) wanting to be expressed that are competing against each other? Explain:

_____

_____

_____

Is there a "strengths synergy" within you or between you and your partner that might be brought forth? In other words, how might a strengths synergy bring balance to the situation?

_____

_____

_____

Growing Together

Suzann Pileggi and James Pawelski (2018), authors of a book on positive psychology and relationships, look back to Aristotle's writings in ancient Greece to highlight three types of friendships: friendships for usefulness (such as a business partnership); friendships for pleasure (having fun with someone); and friendships based on goodness in which the two people value each other's character and attempt to help each other grow in healthy directions. They assert that not just friendships but also close relationships and romantic relationships can function as this third type in a mutually beneficial way. This is how I view the "growing together" element of this model—the use of character strengths to make each other better.

Birds of the Same Feather or Opposites Attract?

In your intimate relationship, look at your VIA Survey profiles (your rank order of strengths from 1 to 24) side by side. Examine your top seven strengths and your partner's top seven strengths. Those you have in common are your *shared strengths,* and those that you don't have in common are your *unique strengths.* It's likely that both types are what previously attracted you to them—and may continue to attract you to them. As the sayings go, "Birds of a feather flock together" and "Opposites attract." Part of growing in strength together is to celebrate and build upon the synergies of the shared strengths and to acknowledge and make the most of the unique strengths. This worksheet will help you make the most of these similarities and differences.

Your top seven strengths:

_____

_____

_____

_____

_____

_____

_____

Your partner's top seven strengths:

_____

_____

_____

_____

_____

_____

_____

Circle the shared strengths above. In what situations do you each use these strengths in synergy? Are there other situations you might create in which you both can express these shared strengths?

_____

_____

_____

_____

Place a star next to the unique strengths of both you and your partner above. In what situations does your partner bring forth these strengths strongly? How does it help your relationship or family?

_____

_____

_____

_____

In what situations do you bring forth *your* unique strengths strongly? How does it help your relationship or your family?

_____

_____

_____

_____

How might the two of you work to notice, appreciate, and encourage each other's shared and unique strengths?

_____

_____

_____

_____

Growth Is an Ongoing Process, Strengths Are the Spark

The strength of curiosity has been found in research studies to build intimacy (Kashdan et al. 2011). It's easy to let curiosity for your partner erode. The truth is, there will always be so much we don't know about our partner. Why not try to keep the curiosity kindled? How might you use your curiosity for your partner more?

_____

_____

_____

It's special to have positive rituals that you and your partner can reliably do together, like an annual couples retreat, a monthly date night, or reading in bed together before sleep. What are your positive rituals? If you can't think of any, talk with your partner about creating a shared, meaningful, positive experience.

_____

_____

_____

How might you use your character strengths to help your relationship focus on the good? This might be the "greater good" of helping others, your neighborhood, or society in some way, or it could be goodness in terms of finding ways for you and your partner to stay focused on expressing your character strengths, the best parts of yourselves, in the relationship.

_____

_____

_____

It's human nature to complain when things go wrong, but it's empowering for your relationship to reflect on what goes right. Make a regular date—over Monday-morning coffee or a Sunday-night recap session—to talk with your partner about what went right in the past week. No matter how bad the week, there are always positives to discover and strengths that were used. Set a plan to take regular action with your partner to spend time reflecting on what's right:

_____

_____

_____

Learn. Practice. SHARE.

Creating positive and healthy relationships by using your own strengths and championing the strengths of others is a rich and deep area of exploration. Spend some extra time studying and practicing the activities in this chapter.

As you review, what stands out most to you? Who will be the first three people with whom you can practice some of these relationship-building activities?

_____

_____

_____

_____

_____

_____

CHAPTER 8

Engage the Present Moment to Build Confidence and Resilience

Here's an experiment you can try right now. Go to your kitchen cabinet and get a clear jar (or clear cup) with a lid. Fill the bottom with an inch of dirt or mud. Fill the rest of the jar with water. Seal the jar and shake well. Notice what happens. The water becomes cloudy and difficult to see through, right? Place the jar down for a few moments. The dirt eventually settles and the water becomes clear again.

Our mind is like the jar. Stress is the dirt or mud. When stress builds and builds and you don't use your strengths or other tools to handle it, your mind becomes cloudy, overwhelmed. You become unfocused, short-tempered, tense, disengaged, upset, and more susceptible to your bad habits and vices.

Mindfulness offers a counterbalance. Mindfulness means to see things clearly—to see things as they are. To notice the details of your present moment, to experience your senses, to actually "be" here as opposed to "do, do, do." If you breathe and focus your attention on the present moment, your mind becomes clearer and steadier, yet active and engaged. This clarity means you are seeing through the water in the jar *and* you are seeing the mud that remains in the jar. It's not about siphoning out the mud (or stress) to eliminate it. Rather, you are seeing the whole picture with fresh eyes.

Character strengths also lead to such clarity. They give us perspective, authenticity, and energy to transform the moment—to understand the water while not getting lost within the dirt. We tap into our strength of self-regulation to manage our impulses in the present moment, curiosity to see things differently, creativity to build the new, and kindness and humility to attend to others at any moment.

This chapter brings together these two powerful concepts of mindfulness and character strengths. Research is showing this to be a powerful synergy (Niemiec 2012, 2014; Niemiec,

Rashid, and Spinella 2012) that generates numerous benefits for well-being and positive out-comes (Ivtzan, Niemiec, and Briscoe 2016; Niemiec and Lissing 2016; Pang and Ruch 2018).

As your mindfulness grows in the present moment, so too will your confidence to handle challenging moments. Consequently, your resilience, your capacity to bounce back from future stressors, builds.

In order to engage your mindfulness and character strengths more in the present moment, you first need to consider what kinds of experiences you have during your day. These can be categorized into three broad types: pleasant experiences, unpleasant experiences, and mundane or neutral experiences. Each presents an important opportunity for growth, so let's explore them a little closer, including an activity and a strengths-based meditation for each.

The Pleasant: Noticing and Growing Your Positives with Perspective

Blind spots are part of life. We all miss details when it comes to knowing ourselves and what's best in us. I refer to this as *strengths blindness,* and it can be an underlying stressor because we don't know what we don't know. If someone doesn't realize they're a particularly angry person or that they never seem to smile—and if no one points this out to them—they have no idea how many people have noticed this and avoided them or trusted them less or felt less comfortable around them.

We're very sensitive to our weaknesses and the criticisms of others and want to keep improving on any blind spots we have about our problems. But we seem to be less focused on becoming aware of the blind spots we have about our positive qualities and pleasant experiences. Mindfulness has been shown to be an important mechanism in overcoming blind spots in how we see ourselves (Carlson 2013). It's an opportunity to deepen our self-awareness and, in turn, our well-being in and connectedness to the world around us.

A common blind spot around the positive is the struggle to receive compliments from others. Are you mindful of the good things people say about you? Awareness of compliments can be especially insightful and offer you opportunity for growth.

Chances are, if you're feeling down or low in self-confidence, you either don't notice a compliment someone gives you or you are quick to discount or minimize the importance or meaning of the compliment. In other words, you may render the compliment useless. Mindful awareness of compliments is about clearly seeing and hearing what others say. Rather than listening to only the inner negative critic, you can learn to hear the good too.

Mindfulness of Compliments

The following short activity has been shown in research studies to not only boost confidence and resilience, but also to build feelings of security in one's relationship over both the short and the long run (Marigold, Holmes, and Ross 2007, 2010). Although these questions originally applied to intimate relationships, you can also answer them with a boss or friend in mind.

Name a compliment you received from an important person in your life:

_____

_____

Why did this person admire you? Describe what the compliment meant to you and its significance for your relationship with them:

_____

_____

_____

What specific character strength(s) was your partner seeing and appreciating in you with this compliment (even if they didn't use the exact language of the VIA Classification at the time)?

_____

_____

_____

Mindfulness of This Moment and the Immediate Future Moment

Another way to take more notice of the pleasant experiences in life is to slow down, pause, and breathe. It's amazing the amount of detail we begin to take in when we come to our senses and breathe in the present moment. There's a story of a young woman who jogged every day up one side of a slightly sloping hill and then down the other side. Week after week, she jogged with a green valley along her right or her left. One day, her ankle was bothering her so she had to walk instead. On that walk, she suddenly noticed all these tiny purple flowers growing up and down the hill she'd never seen before. What else wasn't she seeing? Only by slowing down did she have the chance to notice the wider reality of her present moment. There are times when you need to run through life (multitasking to get things done), but there are times when it's best to walk through life too, to stop and breathe.

You've had many moments where you've experienced pleasure—alone and with others. Mindfulness gets you in the doorway to notice the pleasure. Then it's your character strengths that widen your perspective to stay with the pleasure and experience it further or shift to something else. To help you solidify this combination of mindfulness and character strengths in pleasant moments, I suggest you use a *gatha*, which is a short verse or poetic expression that brings your attention fully into the present moment *and* to the immediate future moment.

Here's a popular gatha I often use to deepen my awareness of pleasurable experiences, such as watching my children play or eating a nice meal. It was created by the luminary mindfulness teacher Thich Nhat Hanh (1979):

Breathing in, I calm my body.

Breathing out, I smile.

Dwelling in this present moment

I know this is a wonderful moment.

As you say these words with attentiveness (with eyes open or closed), you'll probably notice a physiological benefit (from focusing your muscles on breathing and smiling), a psychological benefit (from the statements of well-being), and a sense of perspective building (from the reminder of "dwelling" in the moment, which is a "wonderful" moment).

Another gatha specific to your character strengths (Niemiec 2014) may reveal similar benefits for you:

Breathing in, I see my strengths.

Breathing out, I value my strengths.

Dwelling now, in my strengths,

I express myself fully.

The practice is to memorize the four lines of either gatha, then say them to yourself as you pair each alternating line with your in-breath and your out-breath. So when you're having a pleasant experience—when you notice you are in the midst of a meaningful conversation, when you are observing several birds at play outside your window, or when you are savoring the smile on a loved one's face—say a gatha to yourself. You'll find yourself coming more deeply into the moment and appreciating it as it's happening, rather than as a memory afterward. And the more you practice with these gathas, the more you'll take notice of and appreciate the pleasant experiences in your life!

Meditation: Mindfulness and Strengths Gathas

The audio form of these gathas takes the above discussion to an even deeper sensory level. You can listen to them at http://www.newharbinger.com/42808.

Once you begin this practice, answer the following questions to build insight and enhance your mindfulness.

Write about your experience using one of the gathas:

_____

_____

_____

_____

_____

What is it like to recite a gatha in the midst of a pleasant experience?

_____

_____

_____

_____

_____

Gathas do not have to be limited to pleasant experiences. In fact, they are very effective in unpleasant situations as well. As you become comfortable with each gatha, practice using them at times of stress too. You'll find each can be helpful in a wide range of situations.

The Unpleasant: Bravely Face and Reframe Your Struggles

Unpleasant moments and situations are another natural part of our day. But notice that I call them "unpleasant," not "negative." That's because the word "negative" conjures up something that is bad or unproductive. In reality, unpleasant experiences can be very productive, as they can create learning opportunities, build meaning, and bring out the best in us. In other words, they can catalyze our strengths. As Dan Goleman (1997) explains based on his conversations with the Dalai Lama, such experiences might create "afflictive" emotions like sadness, anxiety, and anger. Afflictive emotions can be motivating to help you take action and improve yourself.

Let's take an obvious example of an unpleasant experience: failure. Nobody likes to fail at something. But one thing that experts agree on is that failure is necessary for growth. We can embrace it, learn from it, and see the good in it. Easier said than done, I know, especially when you're in the throes of disappointment and feelings of helplessness and hopelessness that failure can bring.

So it takes our character strengths to view failure differently—the perspective to step back, the self-regulation to shift away from negative automatic thoughts that flood our mind, the love of learning to pursue new knowledge, and the perseverance to keep up that new knowledge, to name just a few.

Mindfulness of failure helps us learn. We can feel squashed by failure and give up, or we can view failure as a learning opportunity. Prominent authors in building confidence have observed that the most important response to failure is to take action, to leave your comfort zone (Kay and Shipman 2014). This is because we need action in order to grow. We need to take risks and struggle in order to build the confidence that we can succeed.

Another author on self-confidence, Louisa Jewell (2017), agrees but observes that it's not confidence that you need in order to do something new. After all, how can you have confidence in something you've never done? Rather, it is bravery, courage. Putting the strength of bravery into action boosts confidence. And even though bravery is not a strength that many people commonly rank high on, it is a capacity that is available to anyone. According to strengths pioneer and author Robert Biswas-Diener (2012), your willingness to act must be greater than your fear—that's the prerequisite for expressing the strength of bravery.

Research shows that you can activate your bravery and your willingness to take meaningful action in the face of adversity in a number of ways. One is to label courageous experiences—that is, to spot bravery in yourself or to spot it in others if you're trying to help them muster more courage (Hannah, Sweeney, and Lester 2007). In addition to strengths-spotting, another strategy is to focus on the outcomes of a courageous act, such as thinking of the person you're helping, reminding yourself of the goodness of the action, or feeling an obligation to act (Pury 2008).

Build Your Courage

Practice putting this courage research into action with an unpleasant experience in your life.

Name an unpleasant experience in which you'd like to be able to take action (or more action):

_____

_____

As you think about this unpleasant experience, list some possible positive outcomes of expressing courage in the face of it:

_____

_____

Think back to a time when you acted bravely during a similar challenge. If you can't think of a similar challenge, then recall here *any* time you've expressed your bravery relatively strongly:

_____

_____

How did it feel to act courageously in the past?

_____

_____

What was going on in your mind when you acted with courage? What were some of the courageous thoughts you had? What thoughts motivated you to be brave?

_____

_____

Finally, look back over your answers to these questions and reflect on how you might use these insights to take courageous action in the future to benefit others.

Positive Reappraisal of the Unpleasant

Facing unpleasant situations can be done with mindfulness and with courageous action, but it can also be handled with a classic psychological approach called *reframing,* or *positive reappraisal.* Even though this precise terminology hasn't always been used in this book so far, you've been employing this strategy all along as you learn ways to reappraise stress through a strengths-based lens. A fun little story will help us now turn our attention more directly to reframing stress and unpleasant situations.

A few years ago, a colleague told me about how her friends—a young couple with a two-year-old son—handled a challenging situation that occurred over the weekend. One morning while the couple was busy doing household chores, the boy got hold of some permanent markers that were on the kitchen table. Grabbing several of them, he walked right over to a wall in their family room and scribbled all over it. When the parents saw what was happening, they were aghast. They looked at each other, exchanged a few words, and made a decision. They went to their local crafts store, purchased a picture frame large enough to encapsulate the scribble, and mounted the frame to the wall, just two feet from the floor. Their home now featured their child's "artwork."

This couple quite literally "reframed" a situation that would normally elicit anger, frustration, and blaming. Instead, they viewed the episode through a different lens and expressed their character strengths (appreciation of beauty, curiosity, perspective, self-regulation) to take a different approach.

Let's practice positive reappraisal with an activity that has been shown to bring a host of benefits, such as increased forgiveness, gratitude, positive emotions, and lessened muscle tension (McCullough, Root, and Cohen 2006; Witvliet et al. 2010).

Start by thinking of a minor conflict or stressful situation you are having with another person. This should be an unpleasant situation in which you feel slightly offended—perhaps you've been overlooked by them, heard them say a negative comment about you, or feel hurt or frustrated by something they're doing.

Briefly describe this situation:

_____

_____

_____

_____

What character strengths did you show at the time of the offense? How did you express them? What character strengths are you showing right now?

_____

_____

_____

_____

What insights have you gained from this offense? In other words, what have you learned from the experience? What meaning can you take from it?

_____

_____

_____

_____

See the complex humanity of this person, a human being who has both flaws and strengths. Like all of us, this person is in need of experiencing positive growth and transformation. What character strengths do you see in the person, however small?

_____

_____

_____

_____

Meditation: A Positive Reappraisal Using Strengths

Meditation is another way to practice positive reappraisal. This meditation invites you to imagine a minor stressor or problem and gives you strategies for reframing it from the perspective of character strengths to give it a fresh look. In an eight-week program on mindfulness-based strengths that I created and deliver (Niemiec 2014), this is a favorite activity of many participants.

Listen to the Positive Reappraisal Using Strengths Meditation at http://www.newharbin ger.com/42808.

Explore a situation in which you use this meditation to reframe a stressor. What do you notice? What strengths did you call forth?

_____

_____

The Mundane: Grow Your Curiosity During Routines

The third type of experiences that comprise our day isn't all that different from the second type, since, let's face it, most people view the mundane chores and boring daily routines of life as unpleasant. As such, some of the topics here will align with those above—as does the research on mindfulness. Consider:

A group of researchers randomly split fifty-one people into two groups: one read a passage on mindful dishwashing before setting to the task of washing dishes; the other read a general dishwashing procedure passage and then proceeded to wash dishes as well (both without the aid of a dishwashing machine). The researchers found that those in the first group had increases in inspiration, curiosity, and overall mindfulness, as well as a decrease in nervousness (Hanley et al. 2015). Isn't that interesting? When the study subjects were guided to engage their senses and be present only to the task at hand, simultaneously letting go of such mental questions as "What's next?" or "What else can I do while I wash dishes?" various benefits emerged.

This is an example of *mindful living,* of bringing mindful attention to whatever you are doing, even the most mundane of tasks, such that any action you are taking can become the focus of your mindfulness of the present moment and an opportunity to use your strengths (Niemiec 2012). You can be "mindful" about literally anything—driving to work, walking down steps, eating lunch, feeding your pet. When you are, it works against your mind going on autopilot, which is when you lose touch with the present moment.

Think of any activity you've done hundreds or even thousands of times, like taking a shower. It's unlikely that you stay in the present moment and attend to the details of the routine because you've done it so often; in fact, present moments last, on average, only three to four seconds (Stern 2004). But we can train the mind to be more mindful, to return to the present moment when it wanders. Scores of studies over the last few decades have shown the advantages of mindfulness to well-being (Sedlmeier et al. 2012).

Let's look at another research-based example of applying mindfulness to the mundane. Harvard scientist Ellen Langer (1989) conducted a study in which she randomly divided people into two groups, asking both to do an activity they did not like (vacuuming, dusting, and so on). Only one of the two groups, however, was given the added instruction to pay attention to three novel features of the activity while doing it. Those who chose watering the plants, for instance, might focus on the vibrancy of the contrasting colors, the weight of the watering can in the hand, and the sound of the water pouring out and hitting the soil. When the groups reported back to the experimenter, Langer discovered that those who were asked to do the boring activity with curiosity (noticing novel qualities of the task) not only ended up enjoying the activity more, but actually engaged in the activity more on their own after the experiment was over!

Mindfulness to Transform a Routine Activity

Let's return to the table of routine activities in chapter 2, in which you examined the character strengths you bring to everyday tasks. Only now you'll examine how you might also apply mindful attention to these activities by calling on your curiosity. This strength helps you pursue novelty and experience all of life's nuances with a sense of newness. Following the sample entry given here, fill in this table to connect your daily rituals to your mindfulness and character strengths.

Routine Activity	How You Can Bring Mindfulness to the Activity	Character Strength(s) Used
Washing your hair	*I feel my fingers scrubbing and making contact with the softness of my hair. I notice the scent of the shampoo for longer than one whiff. I attend to the circular motion of my hands.*	*Prudence; curiosity*
Rising to your alarm clock		
Brushing your teeth		
Driving to work		
Making your lunch		
E-mailing a coworker or friend		
Posting something to social media		

Routine Activity	How You Can Bring Mindfulness to the Activity	Character Strength(s) Used
Talking with a family member		
Eating a snack		
Reading a book, magazine, or online article		
Walking around your neighborhood		
Other activity:		

Meditation: Transform Any Moment with the Character Strengths Breathing Space

The character strengths breathing space is a short meditation that highlights the use of three of your character strengths, which also happen to lie at the heart of virtually any good mindfulness practice:

1. *Curiosity:* Opening your awareness to taking notice of anything you perceive in your present moment—within you and outside of you. During this phase, it's helpful to ask, "What else?" In other words, rather than getting caught up in the details of any

feeling, sensation, mind story, smell, or sound, remind yourself to stay curious by asking, "What else might I notice and discover in my present moment?"

2. *Self-Regulation:* During this phase, the focus is on feeling your in-breath and out-breath, and when your mind wanders, which it will, you gently return your attention back to your breath, over and over. The phrase "Always back to the breath" is a helpful reminder to regulate your very normal, wandering mind.

3. *Perspective:* This phase involves widening your attention to the big picture—staying focused on the sensations of your breathing, yes, but expanding outward to feel your "whole body" as a unified entity. At this point of the meditation, you move from noticing small details to an awareness of the wider view using your strength of perspective.

Listen to the Character Strengths Breathing Space Meditation at http://www.newharbin ger.com/42808.

When will you set a time to conduct this character strengths breathing space meditation—as you wake up and are lying in bed, while showering, over your lunch break, when you first get in your car?

_____

_____

What do you notice about your character strengths of curiosity, self-regulation, and perspective during this practice? Do you notice other strengths as well?

_____

_____

_____

Learn. Practice. SHARE.

In this chapter, we talked about the various kinds of experiences you have throughout your day and how your mindfulness and character strengths can help you engage more deeply with any of them, sometimes even transform them. As you deepen your mindfulness practice to become more present in the moment, you will develop a new appreciation for the pleasant experiences in life, you will grow from the unpleasant experiences, and you will revitalize your mundane experiences. This brings newfound confidence and stress resilience.

Consider what you learned in this chapter and the meditations and practices it presented. What seems to be most important for you right now? Whom will you share it with? Would it make sense for you to engage in a practice, discussion, or activity in this chapter with someone else?

_____

_____

_____

_____

_____

CHAPTER 9

Find Meaning and Spread Goodness

Are you ready for a challenge called the "deathbed test"? I know it sounds rather morbid, but it's a very impactful exercise worth the effort. Here goes: imagine you are lying on your death-bed and you're asked to complete these two statements:

I wish I would have spent more time _____.

Looking back on my life, I'm very proud that I _____.

Reflect on your answers. What stands out to you about either of them?

_____

_____

_____

Based on your responses, what action(s) would be helpful to take now in your life?

_____

_____

_____

Now infuse character strengths into each. How might you use particular strengths to realize the wish you noted in the first statement?

_____

_____

_____

What strengths are involved in what you noted you're most proud of?

_____

_____

_____

Research studies have shown that exercises like this, which remind us that time is scarce and limited, nurture our well-being (Kurtz 2008; Layous et al. 2018). Although it's a bit uncomfortable on some level to imagine the end of our lives, the insights and meaning generated can be invaluable.

So let's try another exercise in the same vein, called "What Matters Most?" The three simple words of this question are also packed with substance and meaning.

What matters most to you in this one life you have? Give this serious question some serious thought, and write down what you come up with here:

_____

_____

_____

_____

The next question then becomes: Can you have what matters most to you, can you acquire it, maintain it, create it, attain this goal or goals *without* using your character strengths? The answer is you cannot. It doesn't matter what you named—being happy, raising happy kids, having a healthy family, increasing the well-being of others, reaching particular life achievements, building a good relationship, finding inner peace, improving the environment, or making a meaningful contribution to society. For each of these life values, multiple character strengths are integral.

Explore the character strengths that are necessary pathways to building or maintaining what you identified as being most important to you in your life:

_____

_____

_____

_____

These two activities may have led to the same place for you. Or they may have produced very different responses. Either is okay. The important thing is, each plays a critical role in your sense of meaning in life. Considering the "big questions" like this helps to form the bedrock of meaning. If you can get clear on what matters most to you and then create pathways for reaching and maintaining it, if you live a life you can be proud of that isn't filled with regrets about what you didn't make time for, then you'll have a sustainable source of meaning. And this can be a fountain of well-being for yourself and others.

The Three Types of Meaning

The science of meaning has made substantial strides in recent years. Interestingly, stress and meaning often go hand in hand. Scientists have found that stress is strongly and positively linked with meaning in life. Stress has been found—repeatedly—to predict a greater sense of meaning. The higher the number of stressful life events people have experienced in the past, the greater the meaning they feel. And the higher the amount of stress people experience in the present, the more likely they are to report that their life is meaningful (Baumeister et al. 2013).

When you go through the challenges of stress—the physical and psychological difficulties of it, as well as the threat of uncertainty and the unknown that stress often brings—you likely take something substantial from that experience. You see life with greater perspective, you feel that those stressors were not suffered in vain, that they meant something important, and you feel different in some way. Though the process of successfully navigating stress can seem vague when we are actually going through it in the moment, it's all part of the experience of meaning.

By studying the work of philosophers, theologians, educators, and scientists over the centuries, researchers have been able to break meaning down into three types (Martela and Steger 2016):

1. *Coherence:* making sense of life (thinking-oriented)

2. *Significance:* sensing life's value, that it's worth living (feeling-oriented)

3. *Purpose:* having a particular life direction, goals and aims in life (behavior-oriented)

Breaking meaning down in this way can help you better understand your own level of it and discover where you are strong and where you could use a lift. Taken together, these three types of meaning represent a full psychology—your thoughts, feelings, and behaviors that underlie what is meaningful to you.

Researchers are also making strides in discovering which character strengths are most highly connected with meaning. The strengths that are rising to the top are curiosity, perspective, social intelligence, appreciation of beauty, gratitude, and spirituality (Wagner et al. 2018). These six strengths in particular may provide a direct pathway for you to create more life meaning. Of course, another pathway is to turn to your signature strengths and consider how one of them might help you establish more coherence, greater significance, or more purpose in your life.

Finding Meaning in the Little Things

Although we can discover meaning in big things (having a child, overcoming cancer), there are moments in every hour of every day in which we can discover meaning. We can look to our daily routines (sipping coffee while gazing at trees in our backyard) and simple interactions (the smile of a child in the grocery store) to discover meaning. These, too, help us make sense of life, feel the value of life, and point us toward purposeful action.

Take a look at one part of your day—the morning, afternoon, or evening—and examine it for little dosages of meaning. Describe one of the "little things" that was meaningful during that part of your day:

_____

_____

_____

What character strengths are part of this meaningful experience? Pay particular attention to the strengths of curiosity, perspective, spirituality, and appreciation of beauty. Also, look to your signature strengths.

_____

_____

_____

As you explore smaller moments of meaning, which of the types of meaning (making sense of things in life; feeling the significance of life; directing your life in a purposeful way) are you tapping into? Describe:

_____

_____

_____

Take a look at another part of your day. This time, look specifically for *interpersonal meaning*. Look for any small interaction you had with someone that was in some way meaningful to you. It may be as small as a gesture or other nonverbal expression or a short conversation. Describe the experience:

_____

_____

_____

What character strengths are part of this meaningful experience?

_____

_____

_____

As you explore interpersonal moments of meaning, which of the types of meaning (making sense of things in life; feeling the significance of life; directing your life in a purposeful way) are you tapping into? Describe:

_____

_____

_____

You might have noticed as you explore these moments of your life that, in reality, the little things are not little. They're big. They're life—life and meaning emerging out of your present moment.

Going Beyond Personal Meaning

Your strengths equate to your ultimate human potential. What would it be like if you enacted your highest potential with your strengths? Tapped into your energy for meaning and purpose and unleashed your strengths outward for the greater good? What if everyone in your family took this approach? Everyone in your city? Think of the positive synergy that would unfold. Indeed, it would fill the world with more character, virtue, and strength.

But it starts with each one of us.

The starting point is simple: be good and spread goodness.

Research in positive psychology has made it clear that doing good things for people helps ourselves and others (Peterson 2006). Deliberately spreading goodness in the world is a way to manage stress by building your strength resources. There are an infinite number of ways you can spread goodness. As emphasized throughout this book, there are many paths to using your strengths to reach particular personal outcomes or to positively impact others. One pathway you always have available is to turn to your signature strengths, regardless of which strengths those are. You can use your social intelligence to respond with excitement to someone's good news, extend gratitude to someone because they inspire you, and offer forgiveness to someone who has wronged you. Whatever your signature strengths are, bring them forth to benefit others and your community. The ripple effect will be felt.

Another simple way to be good and spread goodness is to express your strength of kindness, which is consistently one of the most common strengths people report across the globe (McGrath 2015; Park, Peterson, and Seligman 2004). Kindness breeds kindness—it creates a "pay it forward" phenomenon—and the benefits of random acts of kindness to well-being have been evidenced in various studies (Pressman, Kraft, and Cross 2015). Unselfish kindness offered solely to benefit others is stronger than kindness offered out of self-interest (Baker and Bulkley 2014). Kind acts have been shown to cascade through social networks, affecting numerous people with one act of goodness (Fowler and Christakis 2010).

Your strength of kindness has many facets, as shown by the wide range of examples in the following table. Although the types overlap to a degree, each offers a distinct way of viewing your strength of kindness.

Type of Kindness	Example(s)
Kind acts	Acts of service; random acts of kindness in your community; paying kindness forward
Compassion	Deeply "feeling with" the suffering of another; really being there with the person to offer understanding and your presence
Generosity	Offering money as well as time to those in need
Care	Showing support and thoughtfulness to those in need; visiting someone who is sick; helping others understand that they "matter" to you
Nurturance	Tending to the specific needs of someone who is sick; offering sustenance (food, water, hugs) to those in need
Being nice and friendly	Simple cordial greetings; offering the gift of conversation; helping others feel welcomed

What does "being good" mean to you?

_____

_____

_____

_____

Which type of kindness listed in the table resonates most with you? Why?

_____

_____

_____

_____

How might you tap into your kindness to express more goodness to others in your family, your community, or your larger society?

_____

_____

_____

_____

You can embody meaning and spread goodness into the world. It's easier than you think. Know your strengths, connect them deeply in your life, and impact others in a positive way, one person at a time.

Learn. Practice. SHARE.

This chapter has been about thinking big—not only for ourselves, but for others and society at large. Big thinking can come from the little. It might come from examining a small moment we take for granted, a casual interaction with someone in which we find meaning, a new idea that we can apply our strengths to and that then ripples outward into the world. It all matters. It's all important. It's all big. And our strengths are embedded in all of it.

What part of this chapter was most important for you? Which idea or theme has the most potential to have a positive impact on your life and the lives of others? Is anything a game changer in terms of how you see yourself in the world?

Share with others—face-to-face, on social media, or in an essay—what is most impactful for you in terms of making meaning and creating goodness. People want to hear your story!

_____

_____

_____

_____

_____

_____

Strengths Transform Stressful Challenges into Opportunities for Growth

You've come a long way! You have journeyed through a wide range of strengths-based activities and reflections on new ways to view and handle stress. I hope you are feeling empowered to turn to your character strengths to create your best life, which entails enhancing your well-being, being productive at work, finding meaning in small moments, elevating positivity in your relationships, and, of course, feeling strong in how you perceive and manage stress.

Applying character strengths is one of the best yet least-known strategies for relieving stress. But you now have the tools for making the most of your character strengths. Your skills with strengths will improve with practice. This will create stronger relationships, families, and communities.

Your Favorite Activities and Best Insights

Take a moment to log your personal highlights of this workbook. Skim back over the chapters to see what stands out most for you—your most meaningful explorations, the most effective activities, your most impactful insights. What takeaways are going to inspire you the most going forward? What brought forth either a large or small shift in your thinking, feeling, or behavior? There's space for ten entries, but feel free to keep going on a separate page.

Best Insights	Why Is This Insight Important for You?	Favorite Activities	How Did You Apply This Activity?	How Does This Activity Help You or Others?
Stress can be viewed as helpful rather than as always harmful.	It transforms how I think about my kids and the stress that comes with being a busy, working parent.	The sharing portion at the end of each chapter.	For each chapter, I posted two of my learnings on Facebook and sat down with my spouse to talk about what each chapter was about.	I feel a sense of wellness when I share my positive experiences and ideas, and it helps me to see others get excited and say they will try it out too.

Best Insights	Why Is This Insight Important for You?	Favorite Activities	How Did You Apply This Activity?	How Does This Activity Help You or Others?

It can be easy to forget some of our best learnings—especially after we close a book! How will you keep your most valuable insights fresh in your mind? Maybe you can write them down on note cards you carry with you, jot them down on sticky notes you place around your home and workspace, or set up a regular time to talk about one character strength each week with a designated "strengths buddy." Any other ideas?

_____

_____

_____

_____

As you deepen your strengths practice, your insights will continue to grow and your responses to the various exercises will continue to evolve. How will you keep up your strengths practice? Will you regularly do some of your favorite activities? How will you remind yourself to maintain your practice?

_____

_____

_____

_____

End Review: What Are Your Stress Levels?

It's time to reassess your stress levels in various situations again, as you did at the beginning of chapter 1 and at the end of chapter 5. Turn back to the rating table in the "What Are Your Stress Levels?" section in the first chapter and fill in the third and final ("End") column with your current levels.

Now that you have data from three different vantage points, have any patterns emerged across the stressors? Big changes, little changes, increases, decreases? As you look at the situations and your changes in stress intensity (or lack thereof) in the face of them, is there anything noteworthy? Explore your observations here:

_____

_____

_____

_____

_____

_____

_____

This Is Not the End

Learning from stress, appreciating the importance of stress, building tools to manage stress—each is a lifelong process. You learn, move two steps forward, you forget, move one step back, challenge yourself, and move two steps forward again. Understanding this clearly—recognizing that there is mud in your jar but also clarity in the water—helps you strive forward.

Spotting and valuing character strengths in yourself and others, applying them to problematic stressors, using them in the complexities of your personal and your work life as you seek meaning—these, too, are processes to enhance your life. You ride the wave, face down the wave, swim along with the wave, and are sometimes knocked down by the wave. Still, through it all, you turn to your character strengths, which are always there waiting for you. It's up to you to bring mindfulness and intentionality to them.

Many people benefit from rereading, rewriting, redoing, rediscussing many aspects of this character strengths practice program. The feedback I receive on my courses, workshops, and publications tells me that people find value in the "repeating"—that the depth potential of character strengths work is virtually endless. So I encourage you to return to any part of this workbook that speaks to you at any point in time with a particular challenge you're facing. You'll likely find something new and helpful to apply to it.

It has been a privilege to lead you through these character strengths practices. I appreciate the effort you have put forth. I know it can sometimes be simultaneously challenging and interesting, both stressful and meaningful, both ordinary and transformative. Keep at it. Keep up this work as a conscious part of your life. After all, these strengths are in you and of you—they *are* you. Keep your unique self engaged and in service to others. In many ways, the world is depending on you to do so.

I wish you well on your journey. May you bring your character strengths forth to help guide you through the peaks and valleys of life and all the spaces in between.

Acknowledgments

Thank you to the special and talented team of the VIA Institute on Character. First off, to Neal Mayerson, who handed me this book project and had the confidence in me to see it through strongly. Neal's vision and innovation for the advancement of character strengths is uncanny, unselfish, and unparalleled. Deep bows of appreciation also go to Kelly Aluise and Breta Cooper, as well as to Donna Mayerson, whose thinking and collaboration were instrumental in giving final shape to chapter 7. Thanks also to other collegial stars—Chris, Jeff, Maureen, and Clare. If not for the whole VIA team working to advance these concepts, to understand and apply the research, and to distill these into best practices for multiple audiences, there would be no book.

Thank you to the entire New Harbinger team, who believed in this idea of bringing the science of character strengths into a user-friendly workbook format that offers a new vision for stress management. Special thanks to Wendy Millstine, for initiating the idea and building my assurance that it can and *should* be done; to Jess O'Brien, for sustaining this confidence and holding the torch along the way; to Jennifer Holder, for her brilliant editing that helped me transform my style while keeping the writing authentic; and to Cindy Nixon, my prudently precise and caring copy editor.

Thank you to my friends and colleagues in positive psychology, a handful of whom I was active with during the writing of this book, including Itai, Roger, Dan, Bob, Tayyab, Claudia, Ruth, Willi, James, and everybody else whose names fall within the lines and spaces of their names. You, too, are appreciated.

Thank you to my family, extended family, relatives, neighbors, friends, and the Cincinnati community. Deep gratitude to Mom, Dad, Joey, Lisa, Monica, J.P., Zara, Bob, Gloria, Andy—and, of course, Rachelle, Rhys, Ryland, and my three-year-old, to whom this book is dedicated (R4 x M forever).

Resources on Strengths

Other Books on Character Strengths by Ryan Niemiec

The Power of Character Strengths: Appreciate and Ignite Your Positive Personality (with Robert McGrath, 2019)

Offers stories, key ideas, research tidbits, and a myriad of practical strategies for using each of the 24 character strengths. Includes a popular four-step program called Strengths Builder.

Character Strengths Interventions: A Field Guide for Practitioners (2018)

This is positive psychology's first field guide into character strengths, citing hundreds of studies while offering easy-to-understand, practical models and tools for any helping professional. Includes nearly 100 handouts for practitioner and client use.

Mindfulness and Character Strengths (2014)

Offers a deep integration of how mindfulness improves strengths use and how character strengths support mindful living and meditation. Includes the full manual for leading mindfulness-based strengths practice (MBSP), an eight-week, evidence-based program used by practitioners worldwide.

Positive Psychology at the Movies 2 (with Danny Wedding, 2014)

Discusses over 1,500 movies, analyzed and categorized across the 24 character strengths. Also includes movies that exemplify resilience, mindfulness, meaning, engagement, positive relationships, and achievement.

Particular Domains Using Strengths

Academic text: *Character Strengths and Virtues: A Handbook and Classification* (by Chris Peterson and Martin Seligman, 2004)

Coaching: *Authentic Strengths* (by Fatima Doman, 2016)

General: *30 Days of Character Strengths* (by Jane Anderson, 2018) and *Character Strengths Matter* (by Shannon Polly and Kathryn Britton, 2015)

Parenting: *The Strengths Switch* (by Lea Waters, 2017)

Project management: *Be a Project Motivator* (by Ruth Pearce, 2018)

Romantic relationships: *Happy Together* (by Suzann Pileggi and James Pawelski, 2018)

Work: *Your Strengths Blueprint* (by Michelle McQuaid and Erin Lawn, 2014)

Specific Character Strengths

Creativity: *Wired to Create* (by Barry Scott Kaufman and Carolyn Gregoire, 2015)

Curiosity: *Curious?* (by Todd Kashdan, 2009)

Judgment: *Thinking, Fast and Slow* (by Daniel Kahneman, 2011)

Love of Learning: *The Power of Mindful Learning* (by Ellen Langer, 1997)

Perspective: *Practical Wisdom* (by Barry Schwartz and Kenneth Sharpe, 2011)

Bravery: *The Courage Quotient* (by Robert Biswas-Diener, 2011) and *Psychological Courage* (by Daniel Putnam, 2004)

Perseverance: *Mindset* (by Carol Dweck, 2006)

Honesty/Authenticity: *The Gifts of Imperfection* (by Brené Brown, 2010)

Zest: *The Body and Positive Psychology* (by Kate Hefferon, 2013)

Love: *Love 2.0* (by Barbara Fredrickson, 2013)

Kindness: *Self-Compassion* (by Kristin Neff, 2011)

Social Intelligence: *Social Intelligence* (by Daniel Goleman, 2006)

Teamwork: *Woven* (by Fiona Campbell Hunter, 2017)

Fairness: *The Fairness Instinct* (by L. Sun, 2013)

Leadership: *The Humanitarian Leader in Each of Us* (by Frank LaFasto and Carl Larson, 2012)

Forgiveness: *Beyond Revenge* (by Michael McCullough, 2008)

Humility: *Humility: The Quiet Virtue* (by Everett Worthington, 2007)

Prudence: *Organize Your Mind, Organize Your Life* (by Paul Hammerness and Margaret Moore, 2011)

Self-Regulation: *Willpower* (by Roy Baumeister and John Tierney, 2011)

Appreciation of Beauty & Excellence: *Awe* (by Paul Pearsall, 2007)

Gratitude: *Thanks!* (by Robert Emmons, 2007)

Hope: *Making Hope Happen* (by Shane Lopez, 2014)

Humor: *Humor as Survival Training for a Stressed-Out World* (by Paul McGhee, 2010)

Spirituality: *The Gospel of Happiness* (by Christopher Kaczor, 2015)

References

Baker, W., and N. Bulkley. 2014. "Paying It Forward vs. Rewarding Reputation: Mechanisms of Generalized Reciprocity." *Organization Science* 25(5): 1493–1510. http://doi.org/10.1287/orsc.2014.0920.

Baumeister, R. F., E. Bratslavsky, C. Finkenaeuer, and K. D. Vohs. 2001. "Bad Is Stronger Than Good." *Review of General Psychology* 5(4): 323–370. http://doi.org/10.1037/1089-2680.5.4.323.

Baumeister, R. F., K. D. Vohs, J. L. Aaker, and E. N. Garbinsky. 2013. "Some Key Differences Between a Happy Life and a Meaningful Life." *Journal of Positive Psychology* 8(6): 505–516.

Biswas-Diener, R. 2006. "From the Equator to the North Pole: A Study of Character Strengths." *Journal of Happiness Studies* 7: 293–310. http://doi.org/10.1007/s10902-005-3646-8.

Biswas-Diener, R. 2012. *The Courage Quotient: How Science Can Make You Braver.* San Francisco, CA: Jossey-Bass.

Bryant, F. B., and J. Veroff. 2007. *Savoring: A New Model of Positive Experience.* Mahway, NJ: Lawrence Erlbaum Associates.

Buschor, C., R. T. Proyer, and W. Ruch. 2013. "Self- and Peer-Rated Character Strengths: How Do They Relate to Satisfaction with Life and Orientations to Happiness?" *Journal of Positive Psychology* 8(2): 116–127. http://doi.org/10.1080/17439760.2012.758305.

Carlson, E. N. 2013. "Overcoming the Barriers to Self-Knowledge: Mindfulness as a Path to Seeing Yourself as You Really Are." *Perspectives on Psychological Science* 8(2): 173–186.

Caunt, B. S., J. Franklin, N. E. Brodaty, and H. Brodaty. 2013. "Exploring the Causes of Subjective Well-Being: A Content Analysis of Peoples' Recipes for Long-Term Happiness." *Journal of Happiness Studies* 14(2): 475–499.

Cowden, R. G., and A. Meyer-Weitz. 2016. "Self-Reflection and Self-Insight Predict Resilience and Stress in Competitive Tennis." *Social Behavior and Personality* 44(7): 1133–1150.

Dalton, A. N., and S. A. Spiller. 2012. "Too Much of a Good Thing: The Benefits of Implementation Intentions Depend on the Number of Goals." *Journal of Consumer Research* 39(3): 600–614. http://doi.org/10.1086/664500.

Diener, E., and S. Oishi. 2005. "The Nonobvious Social Psychology of Happiness." *Psychological Inquiry* 16(4): 162–167.

Diener, E., and M. E. P. Seligman. 2004. "Beyond Money Toward an Economy of Well-Being." *Psychological Science in the Public Interest* 5(1): 1–31.

Duhigg, C. 2012. *The Power of Habit: Why We Do What We Do in Life and Business.* New York: Random House.

Emmons, R. A., and M. E. McCullough. 2003. "Counting Blessings Versus Burdens: An Experimental Investigation of Gratitude and Subjective Well-Being in Daily Life." *Journal of Personality and Social Psychology* 84: 377–389.

Fluckiger, C., F. Caspar, M. Grosse Holtforth, and U. Willutzki. 2009. "Working with Patients' Strengths: A Microprocess Approach." *Psychotherapy Research* 19(2): 213–223. http://doi.org/10.1080/10503300902755300.

Fluckiger, C., and M. Grosse Holtforth. 2008. "Focusing the Therapist's Attention on the Patient's Strengths: A Preliminary Study to Foster a Mechanism of Change in Outpatient Psychotherapy." *Journal of Clinical Psychology* 64: 876–890. http://doi.org/10.1002/jclp.20493.

Fowler, H., and N. A. Christakis. 2010. "Cooperative Behavior Cascades in Human Social Networks." *Proceedings of the National Academy of Science* 107: 5334–5338.

Freidlin, P., H. Littman-Ovadia, and R. M. Niemiec. 2017. "Positive Psychopathology: Social Anxiety via Character Strengths Underuse and Overuse." *Personality and Individual Differences* 108: 50–54. http://doi.org/10.1016/j.paid.2016.12.003.

Gable, S. L., H. T. Reis, E. A. Impett, and E. R. Asher. 2004. "What Do You Do When Things Go Right? The Intrapersonal and Interpersonal Benefits of Sharing Positive Events." *Journal of Personality and Social Psychology* 87(2): 228–245. http://doi.org/10.1037/0022-3514.87.2.228.

Gallup. 2013. "State of the American Workplace: Employee Engagement Insights for U.S. Business Leaders." https://news.gallup.com/reports/178514/state-american-workplace.aspx.

Gander, F., R. T. Proyer, W. Ruch, and T. Wyss. 2013. "Strength-Based Positive Interventions: Further Evidence for Their Potential in Enhancing Well-Being and Alleviating Depression." *Journal of Happiness Studies* 14: 1241–1259. http://doi.org/10.1007/s10902-012 -9380-0.

Gardner, H. 1983. *Frames of Mind: The Theory of Multiple Intelligences.* New York: Basic Books.

Goleman, D. 1997. *Healing Emotions: Conversations with the Dalai Lama on Mindfulness, Emotions, and Health.* Boston: Shambhala.

Gollwitzer, P. M., and G. Oettingen. 2013. "Implementation Intentions." In *Encyclopedia of Behavioral Medicine,* edited by M. Gellman and J. R. Turner. New York: Springer.

Gordon, A. M., and S. Chen. 2016. "Do You Get Where I'm Coming From? Perceived Understanding Buffers Against the Negative Impact of Conflict on Relationship Satisfaction." *Journal of Personality and Social Psychology* 110(2): 239–260.

Grant, A. M., J. Frankline, and P. Langford. 2002. "The Self-Reflection and Insight Scale: A New Measure of Private Self-Consciousness." *Social Behavior and Personality* 30(8): 821–836.

Guo, J., Y. Wang, and X. Y. Liu. 2015. "Relation Between Marital Satisfaction and Character Strengths in Young People." *Chinese Mental Health Journal* 29(5): 383–388.

Hanley, A. W., A. R. Warner, V. M. Dehili, A. I. Canto, and E. L. Garland. 2015. "Washing Dishes to Wash the Dishes: Brief Instruction in an Informal Mindfulness Practice." *Mindfulness* 6: 1095. doi: 10.1007/s12671-014-0360-9.

Hannah, S. T., P. J. Sweeney, and P. B. Lester. 2007. "Toward a Courageous Mind-Set: The Subjective Act and Experience of Courage." *Journal of Positive Psychology* 2(2): 129–135. http://doi.org/10.1080/17439760701228854.

Harzer, C., and W. Ruch. 2015. "The Relationships of Character Strengths with Coping, Work-Related Stress, and Job Satisfaction." *Frontiers in Psychology* 6: no. 165. http://doi .org/10.3389/fpsyg.2015.00165.

Harzer, C., and W. Ruch. 2016. "Your Strengths Are Calling: Preliminary Results of a Web-Based Strengths Intervention to Increase Calling." *Journal of Happiness Studies* 17(6): 2237–2256. http://doi.org/10.1007/s10902-015-9692-y.

Hone, L. C., A. Jarden, S. Duncan, and G. M. Schofield. 2015. "Flourishing in New Zealand Workers: Associations with Lifestyle Behaviors, Physical Health, Psychosocial, and

Work-Related Indicators." *Journal of Occupational and Environmental Medicine* 57(9): 973–983. http://doi.org/10.1097/JOM.0000000000000508.

Hudson, N. W., and R. C. Fraley. 2015. "Volitional Personality Trait Change: Can People Choose to Change Their Personality Traits?" *Journal of Personality and Social Psychology* 109(3): 490–507. http://doi.org/10.1037/pspp0000021.

Ivtzan, I., R. M. Niemiec, and C. Briscoe. 2016. "A Study Investigating the Effects of Mindfulness-Based Strengths Practice (MBSP) on Wellbeing." *International Journal of Wellbeing* 6(2): 1–13.

Jewell, L. 2017. *Wire Your Brain for Confidence: The Science of Conquering Self-Doubt.* Toronto: Famous Warrior Press.

Kashdan, T. B., D. V. Blalock, K. C. Young, K. A. Machell, S. S. Monfort, P. E. McKnight, and P. Ferssizidis. 2017. "Personality Strengths in Romantic Relationships: Measuring Perceptions of Benefits and Costs and Their Impact on Personal and Relational Well-Being." *Psychological Assessment* 30(2): 241–258. doi: 10.1037/pas0000464.

Kashdan, T. B., P. E. McKnight, F. D. Fincham, and P. Rose. 2011. "When Curiosity Breeds Intimacy: Taking Advantage of Intimacy Opportunities and Transforming Boring Conversations." *Journal of Personality* 79: 1369–1401.

Kay, K., and C. Shipman. 2014. *The Confidence Code.* New York: HarperCollins Publishers.

Keyes, C. L. M. 2002. "The Mental Health Continuum: From Languishing to Flourishing in Life." *Journal of Health and Social Behavior* 43: 207–222. http://doi.org/10.2307/3090197.

Kurtz, J. L. 2008. "Looking to the Future to Appreciate the Present: The Benefits of Perceived Temporal Scarcity." *Psychological Science* 19: 1238–1241. http://dx.doi.org/10.1111/j .1467-9280.2008.02231.x.

Langer, E. 1989. *Mindfulness.* Reading, MA: Addison-Wesley.

Lavy, S., H. Littman-Ovadia, and Y. Bareli. 2014. "My Better Half: Strengths Endorsement and Deployment in Married Couples." *Journal of Family Issues* 37(12): 1730–1754. doi: 10 .1177/0192513X14550365.

Layous, K., J. Kurtz, J. Chancellor, and S. Lyubomirsky. 2018. "Reframing the Ordinary: Imagining Time as Scarce Increases Well-Being." *Journal of Positive Psychology* 13(3): 301–308. https://doi.org/10.1080/17439760.2017.1279210.

Linley, A. 2008. *Average to A+: Realising Strengths in Yourself and Others.* Coventry, England: CAPP Press.

Marigold, D. C., J. G. Holmes, and M. Ross. 2007. "More Than Words: Reframing Compliments from Romantic Partners Fosters Security in Low Self-Esteem Individuals." *Journal of Personality and Social Psychology* 92: 232–248. http://doi.org/10.1037/00223514.92.2.232.

Marigold, D. C., J. G. Holmes, and M. Ross, M. 2010. "Fostering Relationship Resilience: An Intervention for Low Self-Esteem Individuals." *Journal of Experimental Social Psychology* 46: 624–630. http://doi.org/10.1016/j.jesp.2010.02.011.

Martela, F., and M. F. Steger. 2016. "The Three Meanings of Meaning in Life: Distinguishing Coherence, Purpose, and Significance." *Journal of Positive Psychology* 11(5): 531–545. http://doi.org/10.1080/17439760.2015.1137623.

Mazzucchelli, T. G., R. T. Kane, and C. S. Rees. 2010. "Behavioral Activation Interventions for Well-Being: A Meta-Analysis." *Journal of Positive Psychology* 5(2): 105–121.

McCullough, M. E., L. M. Root, and A. D. Cohen. 2006. "Writing About the Benefits of an Interpersonal Transgression Facilitates Forgiveness." *Journal of Consulting and Clinical Psychology* 74(5): 887–897. http://doi.org/10.1037/0022-006X.74.5.887.

McGonigal, K. 2015. *The Upside of Stress.* New York: Avery.

McGrath, R. E. 2015. "Character Strengths in 75 Nations: An Update." *Journal of Positive Psychology* 10(1): 41–52. http://doi.org/10.1080/17439760.2014.888580.

McQuaid, M., and E. Lawn. 2014. *Your Strengths Blueprint: How to Be Engaged, Energized, and Happy at Work.* Albert Park, Australia: McQuaid Pty. Ltd.

McQuaid, M., and VIA Institute on Character. 2015. "VIA Character Strengths at Work." https://www.viacharacter.org/blog/strengths-at-work/.

Myers, D. 2000. "The Funds, Friends, and Faith of Happy People." *American Psychologist* 55: 56–67.

Nhat Hanh, T. 1979. *The Miracle of Mindfulness: An Introduction to the Practice of Meditation.* Boston: Beacon.

Niemiec, R. M. 2012. "Mindful Living: Character Strengths Interventions as Pathways for the Five Mindfulness Trainings." *International Journal of Wellbeing* 2(1): 22–33. http://doi.org/10.5502/ijw.v2i1.2.

Niemiec, R. M. 2014. *Mindfulness and Character Strengths: A Practical Guide to Flourishing.* Boston: Hogrefe.

Niemiec, R. M. 2018. *Character Strengths Interventions: A Field Guide for Practitioners.* Boston: Hogrefe.

Niemiec, R. M., and J. Lissing. 2016. "Mindfulness-Based Strengths Practice (MBSP) for Enhancing Wellbeing, Life Purpose, and Positive Relationships." In *Mindfulness in Positive Psychology: The Science of Meditation and Wellbeing,* edited by I. Ivtzan and T. Lomas. New York: Routledge.

Niemiec, R. M., T. Rashid, and M. Spinella. 2012. "Strong Mindfulness: Integrating Mindfulness and Character Strengths." *Journal of Mental Health Counseling* 34(3): 240–253. http://doi.org/10.17744/mehc.34.3.34p6328x2v204v21.

Niemiec, R. M., and D. Wedding. 2014. *Positive Psychology at the Movies: Using Films to Build Character Strengths and Well-Being.* 2nd ed. Boston: Hogrefe.

Niemiec, R. M., and A. Yarova. 2018. "Character Strengths and Health: Research Summary (Part 1)." *Chronicle of Advances in Positive Health and Well-Being* 1(1). http://www.ippanetwork.org/positive-health/character-strengths-and-health-research-summary-part-1/.

Oishi, S., E. Diener, and R. E. Lucas. 2007. "The Optimal Level of Well-Being: Can We Be Too Happy?" *Perspectives on Psychological Science* 2: 346–360.

Pang, D., and W. Ruch. 2018. "The Effect of Mindfulness-Based Strengths Practice on Job Satisfaction and Task Performance: The Mediating Role of Strengths Application." Manuscript submitted for publication. [[NH: May be able to update before printing]]

Park, N., C. Peterson, and M. E. P. Seligman. 2004. "Strengths of Character and Well-Being." *Journal of Social & Clinical Psychology* 23: 603–619. http://doi.org/10.1521/jscp.23.5.628.50749.

Park, N., C. Peterson, and M. E. P. Seligman. 2006. "Character Strengths in Fifty-Four Nations and the Fifty US States." *Journal of Positive Psychology* 1(3): 118–129. http://doi.org/10.1080/17439760600619567.

Peterson, C. 2006. *A Primer in Positive Psychology.* New York: Oxford University Press.

Peterson, C., and M. E. P. Seligman. 2004. *Character Strengths and Virtues: A Classification and Handbook.* New York: Oxford University Press and Washington, DC: American Psychological Association.

Pileggi, S. P., and J. O. Pawelski. 2018. *Happy Together: Using the Science of Positive Psychology to Build Love That Lasts.* New York: Penguin.

Pressman, S. D., T. L. Kraft, and M. P. Cross. 2015. "It's Good to Do Good and Receive Good: The Impact of a 'Pay It Forward' Style Kindness Intervention on Giver and Receiver Well-Being." *Journal of Positive Psychology* 10(4): 293–302. http://doi.org/10.1080/17439760.2014.965269.

Proyer, R. T., F. Gander, S. Wellenzohn, and W. Ruch. 2013. "What Good Are Character Strengths Beyond Subjective Well-Being? The Contribution of the Good Character on Self-Reported Health-Oriented Behavior, Physical Fitness, and the Subjective Health Status." *Journal of Positive Psychology* 8(3): 222–232. http://doi.org/10.1080/17439760.2013.777767.

Proyer, R. T., F. Gander, S. Wellenzohn, and W. Ruch. 2015. "Strengths-Based Positive Psychology Interventions: A Randomized Placebo-Controlled Online Trial on Long-Term Effects for a Signature Strengths– vs. a Lesser Strengths–Intervention." *Frontiers in Psychology* 6: no. 456. http://doi.org/10.3389/fpsyg.2015.00456.

Proyer, R. T., W. Ruch, and C. Buschor. 2013. "Testing Strengths-Based Interventions: A Preliminary Study on the Effectiveness of a Program Targeting Curiosity, Gratitude, Hope, Humor, and Zest for Enhancing Life Satisfaction." *Journal of Happiness Studies* 14(1): 275–292. http://doi.org/10.1007/s10902-0129331-9.

Pury, C. L. S. 2008. "Can Courage Be Learned?" In *Positive Psychology: Exploring the Best in People, Volume 1: Discovering Human Strengths,* edited by S. J. Lopez. Westport, CT: Praeger.

Reis, H., S. Smith, C. Carmichael, P. Caprariello, F. Tsai, A. Rodrigues, and M. R. Maniaci. 2010. "Are You Happy for Me? How Sharing Positive Events with Others Provides Personal and Interpersonal Benefits." *Journal of Personality and Social Psychology* 99(2): 311–329. http://doi.org/10.1037/a0018344.

Rostosky, S. S., and E. D. B. Riggle. 2017. "Same-Sex Couple Relationship Strengths: A Review and Synthesis of the Empirical Literature (2000–2016)." *Psychology of Sexual Orientation & Gender Diversity* 4(1): 1–13. http://dx.doi.org/10.1037/sgd0000216.

Rust, T., R. Diessner, and L. Reade. 2009. "Strengths Only or Strengths and Relative Weaknesses? A Preliminary Study." *Journal of Psychology* 143(5): 465-476. http://doi.org/10.3200/JRL.143.5.465-476.

Ryan, R. M., and C. Frederick. 1997. "On Energy, Personality, and Health: Subjective Vitality as a Dynamic Reflection of Well-Being." *Journal of Personality* 65(3): 529–565.

Schmid, D., and G. Colditz. 2014. "Sedentary Behavior Increases the Risk of Certain Cancers." *Journal of the National Cancer Institute* 106(7). https://doi.org/10.1093/jnci/dju206.

Sedlmeier, P., J. Eberth, M. Schwarz, D. Zimmermann, F. Haarig, S. Jaeger, and S. Kunze. 2012. "The Psychological Effects of Meditation: A Meta-Analysis." *Psychological Bulletin* 138(6): 1139–1171.

Seligman, M. E. P. 1999. "The President's Address." *American Psychologist* 54: 559–562.

Seligman, M. E. P. 2011. *Flourish.* New York: Free Press.

Seligman, M. E. P., T. A. Steen, N. Park, and C. Peterson. 2005. "Positive Psychology Progress: Empirical Validation of Interventions." *American Psychologist* 60: 410–421. http://doi.org/10.1037/0003-066X.60.5.410.

Stern, D. N. 2004. *The Present Moment: In Psychotherapy and Everyday Life.* New York: W. W. Norton & Company.

Veldorale-Brogan, A., K. Bradford, and A. Vail. 2010. "Marital Virtues and Their Relationship to Individual Functioning, Communication, and Relationship Adjustment." *Journal of Positive Psychology* 5(4): 281–293.

Wagner, L., F. Gander, R. T. Proyer, and W. Ruch. 2018. "Character Strengths and PERMA: Investigating the Relationships of Character Strengths with a Multidimensional Framework of Well-Being." Manuscript accepted for publication. [[NH: Author will update at proofing stage]]

Witvliet, C. V. O., R. W. Knoll, N. G. Hinman, and P. A. DeYoung. 2010. "Compassion-Focused Reappraisal, Benefit-Focused Reappraisal, and Rumination After an Interpersonal Offense: Emotion-Regulation Implications for Subjective Emotion, Linguistic Responses, and Physiology." *Journal of Positive Psychology* 5(3): 226–242. http://doi.org/10.1080/17439761003790997.

Wood, A. M., P. A. Linley, J. Matlby, T. B. Kashdan, and R. Hurling, R. 2011. "Using Personal and Psychological Strengths Leads to Increases in Well-Being over Time: A Longitudinal Study and the Development of the Strengths Use Questionnaire." *Personality and Individual Differences* 50: 15–19. http://doi.org/10.1016/j.paid.2010.08.004.

Ryan M. Niemiec, PsyD, is a leading figure in the education, research, and practice of character strengths that are found in all human beings. Ryan is education director of the VIA Institute on Character, a global nonprofit organization in Cincinnati, OH, that advances the latest science and practical applications of character strengths. He's an award-winning psychologist, adjunct professor at Xavier University, and annual instructor at the University of Pennsylvania. He was awarded Fellow of the International Positive Psychology Association in 2017.

As a frequent keynote speaker and workshop leader, Ryan has offered several hundred presentations on positive psychology topics across the globe. He is author of several books, including *Character Strengths Interventions* and *Mindfulness and Character Strengths*; and coauthor of *Movies and Mental Illness*, *Positive Psychology at the Movies*, and *The Power of Character Strengths*. He's penned hundreds of articles for the general public on character strengths, and more than eighty scholarly articles and chapters. He lives with his wife and three kids outside Cincinnati, OH. His highest strengths are hope, love, curiosity, honesty, appreciation of beauty, and fairness.

Foreword writer **Neal H. Mayerson, PhD**, is chairman of the VIA Institute. He received his PhD in clinical psychology, and has worked in hospital, community mental health, and private practice settings for fifteen years. As a psychotherapist, he specializes in chronic pain, eating disorders, and couples therapy.

MORE BOOKS *from*
NEW HARBINGER PUBLICATIONS

THE STRESS-PROOF BRAIN

Master Your Emotional Response to
Stress Using Mindfulness
& Neuroplasticity

978-1626252660 / US $17.95

BUDDHA'S BRAIN

The Practical Neuroscience of
Happiness, Love & Wisdom

978-1572246959 / US $18.95

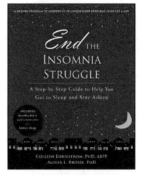

**END THE INSOMNIA
STRUGGLE**

A Step-by-Step Guide to Help You
Get to Sleep & Stay Asleep

978-1626253438 / US $24.95

THE COURAGE HABIT

How to Accept Your Fears, Release
the Past & Live Your Courageous Life

978-1626259874 / US $17.95

**DON'T FEED THE
MONKEY MIND**

How to Stop the Cycle of
Anxiety, Fear & Worry

978-1626255067 / US $16.95

**EMBRACE YOUR
GREATNESS**

Fifty Ways to Build
Unshakable Self-Esteem

978-1684032204 / US $16.95

new harbinger publications
1-800-748-6273 / newharbinger.com

(VISA, MC, AMEX / prices subject to change without notice)

Follow Us

Register your **new harbinger** titles for additional benefits!

When you register your **new harbinger** title—purchased in any format, from any source—you get access to benefits like the following:

- Downloadable accessories like printable worksheets and extra content

- Instructional videos and audio files

- Information about updates, corrections, and new editions

Not every title has accessories, but we're adding new material all the time.

Access free accessories in 3 easy steps:

1. Sign in at NewHarbinger.com (or **register** to create an account).

2. Click on **register a book**. Search for your title and click the **register** button when it appears.

3. Click on the **book cover or title** to go to its details page. Click on **accessories** to view and access files.

That's all there is to it!

If you need help, visit:

NewHarbinger.com/accessories

new harbinger
CELEBRATING
40 YEARS